NOMOS

In support of

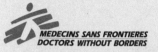

MÉDECINS SANS FRONTIERES
DOCTORS WITHOUT BORDERS

Time for life—with limited edition timepieces in support of Doctors Without Borders/
Médecins Sans Frontières. Each watch raises 100 USD, GBP, or EUR for the Nobel Peace Prize
winning humanitarian organization. And still these handcrafted mechanical watches with the
red 12 cost the same as the classic models from NOMOS Glashütte. Help now, wear forever.

Funds raised are donated to Médecins Sans Frontières USA, UK, or Germany, depending on the specific model purchased. For MSF UK,
the registered charity no. is 1026588. Available at selected retailers in the three participating countries, as well as online. Find your nearest
NOMOS retailer at **nomos-glashuette.com** or order online at **nomos-store.com**.

GRANTA

12 Addison Avenue, London W11 4QR | email editorial@granta.com
To subscribe go to granta.com, or call 020 8955 7011 (free phone 0500 004 033)
in the United Kingdom, 845-267-3031 (toll-free 866-438-6150) in the United States

ISSUE 137: AUTUMN 2016

PUBLISHER AND EDITOR	Sigrid Rausing
DEPUTY EDITOR	Rosalind Porter
POETRY EDITOR	Rachael Allen
ONLINE EDITOR	Luke Neima
ASSISTANT EDITOR	Francisco Vilhena
DESIGNER	Daniela Silva
EDITORIAL ASSISTANTS	Eleanor Chandler, Josie Mitchell
SUBSCRIPTIONS	David Robinson
PUBLICITY	Pru Rowlandson
TO ADVERTISE CONTACT	Kate Rochester, katerochester@granta.com
FINANCE	Morgan Graver
SALES AND MARKETING	Iain Chapple, Katie Hayward
IT MANAGER	Mark Williams
PRODUCTION ASSOCIATE	Sarah Wasley
PROOFS	Katherine Fry, Lesley Levene, Jess Porter, Vimbai Shire
CONTRIBUTING EDITORS	Daniel Alarcón, Anne Carson, Mohsin Hamid, Isabel Hilton, Michael Hofmann, A.M. Homes, Janet Malcolm, Adam Nicolson, Edmund White

National Theatre

A new version of Henrik Ibsen's classic by Patrick Marber, featuring Ruth Wilson.

Travelex £15

Lucian Msamati plays Salieri in a new production of Peter Shaffer's iconic play.

In association with Southbank Sinfonia

A psychological thriller by David Hare, with Hope Davis and Mark Strong.

Produced in association with Scott Rudin

★★★★★
'Something to delight the whole family.'
The Times

Based on the works of JM Barrie. A co-production with Bristol Old Vic

Playing this autumn
South Bank, London SE1

Hedda Gabler photography (Ruth Wilson) by Léa Nielsen, *Amadeus* photography (Lucian Msamati) by Seamus Ryan, *The Red Barn* illustration by Bill Bragg, *Peter Pan* photography by Sam Robinson.

ARTIST you AUTHOR

MFA Visual Narrative
A unique low-residency graduate program in visual
storytelling that combines creative writing and visual arts.
Learn more at **mfavn.sva.edu**

story:visualized
RISOLAB SVA NY

SEA & DEATH

A COLLECTION OF SHORT STORIES EDITED BY SARAH HALL & PETER HOBBS

Featuring:

Ali Smith • Ben Marcus • Kevin Barry • Petina Gappah • Taiye Selasi • Alan Warner • Yiyun Li • Alexander MacLeod • Lynn Coady • Ceridwen Dovey • Robert Drewe • Damon Galgut • Jon McGregor • Guadalupe Nettel • Courttia Newland • Wells Tower • Claire Vaye Watkins • Clare Wigfall

ff

CONTENTS

Introduction

We live near a small park in London. One day last summer there were suddenly hundreds of young people there, staring at their phones, swiping, talking, slowly moving towards something or other – it was like a scene out of Ray Bradbury; a vision of the future. I understood later that they were playing Pokémon GO, and had been brought outside by the hunt, mesmerised by their screens and the merging of the virtual and the real, the old realm of religion.

In this issue, four writers describe growing up in religious sects: Miriam Toews, Matilda Gustavsson, Lauren Hough and Ken Follett. Each of them is marked by their upbringing, from Toews's experience of the emotionally stultifying radical pacifism of the Mennonites to Gustavsson's memories of the eerie false miracles of a Swedish cult and Hough's account of the brutality and neglect of the Family. We end the first part of the issue with international best-selling author Ken Follett, who describes, for the first time, family life with the Plymouth Brethren, a Protestant sect which banned its followers from most forms of 'worldly' pleasures.

'I heard *Another World Is Possible!*', runs a line in Kelly Schirmann's poem 'Your Youth'. But so often the new world turns out more oppressive than the old one. The Russian proverb 'when you cut wood, chips fly' was often quoted in the heyday of Soviet repression, meaning that if you want to achieve a goal you have to make (or inflict) sacrifices. Ivan Chistyakov, whose diary was handed in to Memorial, the Russian human rights organisation dedicated to preserving the memories and history of Soviet Russia, was not a wood chip in that particular sense – on the contrary, he was a perpetrator, a Gulag guard, albeit a reluctant and somewhat sceptical one. He was drafted in the mid-1930s, just as the GULag, the network of forced labour camps, was in a phase of massive expansion, and sent to guard prisoners working on a section of BAM, the Baikal–Amur Mainline Railway.

BAM was originally a civilian project, transferred to GULag control as BAMLag in the early 1930s, when it became clear that it could not be completed with ordinary labour. BAMLag had a vast supply of prisoners and deportees – in 1938 the headcount was some 200,000 people – working under extremely harsh conditions.

Ivan Chistyakov's diary is probably unique: there are few, if any, camp-guard diaries left, not least because being discovered writing such a diary would have been very dangerous. He was, as he expected to be, eventually arrested. Beyond that fact, we know almost nothing about him – we only have a blurred snapshot, with this note: 'Chistyakov, Ivan Petrovich, repressed in 1937–38. Killed at the front in Tula Province in 1941.'

And yet, for all my scepticism about political and religious movements, there are people who would probably be better off in a sect than out on the street. Julie Baird, a San Francisco drug addict, was one of them. Emmanuel Carrère captures photographer Darcy Padilla's engagement with Julie from the early days in San Francisco to the end, when Julie is dying of Aids in a hospital bed in Alaska. I suppose a sect might at least have given her a belief in something other than the dreamy highs of the Ambassador Hotel, that squalid temporary home of San Francisco down-and-outs.

Protest movements are building, on the right and on the left. Perhaps social media is a movement too, with its rules and traditions, its *likes* and *followers*, its candid and benign participants goaded by destructive trolls. By mid-September Pokémon GO had been downloaded 500 million times. What future youth movement might capture them, those international participants in virtual hunts? What do they have in common; what messages might reach them through a game?

The working title of this issue was Followers – but writing about a cult actually implies having left it. Perhaps this issue is about being free rather than about being a follower. ∎

Sigrid Rausing

PEACE SHALL DESTROY MANY

Miriam Toews

In 1962, a young scholar from Saskatchewan by the name of Rudy Wiebe caused outrage and scandal in Mennonite communities throughout North America when he published his first novel, *Peace Shall Destroy Many*. The title, taken from a verse in the Book of Daniel, encapsulated the contention of the novel – that pacifism and non-conflict, core tenets of the Mennonite faith, may in fact be sources of violence and conflict, all the more damaging because unacknowledged or denied.

Although the book was published two years before I was born, I can remember my parents discussing it at the kitchen table, conspiratorially, as if the topic was in itself dangerous. My mother would later tell me that she had driven herself to the city, Winnipeg, the day it was made available in stores – it would never have been sold in my little conservative Mennonite town – to find out what all the fuss was about. By the time I was buying books myself, I had learned to think of this novelist named Rudy Wiebe as controversial and heroic, as an *intellectual* whose work was *groundbreaking* and *revolutionary*. These were exciting words to me.

All the fuss was about the challenging questions posed by the novel's central character, Thom Wiens, an earnest young farmer living in a small isolated community in Saskatchewan (much like the community Rudy Wiebe grew up in). It is 1944, wartime, and the local men have either gone to conscientious objector work camps around Canada, or stayed behind to tend the crops and raise livestock. Wiens begins to wonder whether the Mennonite opposition to war may be self-serving. How can Mennonites stand aside while others are dying to protect the freedoms they enjoy? How can Mennonites justify selling their produce to the Canadian army, at a profit no less, and continue to preach peace and love for one's enemies?

Rudy Wiebe hadn't intended to stir things up with his novel. He was no Mennonite provocateur or self-appointed rabble-rouser. He wanted to write honestly and philosophically about the conflicts that arise from non-conflict. He also wanted to raise questions of sexuality and racism, and to test the established perception of Mennonites as a people '*in* the world but not *of* the world'.

At the time, Wiebe was a devout Christian and respected member of the Mennonite establishment. After the book was published he was fired from his job as the editor of a Mennonite newspaper and denounced, by some, as a liar, an upstart and a traitor. Even worse, an atheist. Others, like my parents, were supportive, secretly though, as was and is the custom among dissenting Mennonites. When my mother said, 'Rudy Wiebe has aired our dirty laundry and it's about time,' she whispered. It was important to keep the peace in all matters, including the matter of *Peace Shall Destroy Many*.

'I guess it was a kind of bombshell,' Wiebe told an interviewer in 1972, 'because it was the first realistic novel ever written about Mennonites in western Canada. A lot of people had no clue how to read it. They got angry. I was talking from the inside and exposing things that shouldn't be exposed.'

Shouldn't be exposed. These are telling words. The conviction that certain realities *shouldn't be exposed* is what lurks behind the time-honoured Mennonite practice of avoiding conflict and refusing engagement. Everyday life in these remote towns and colonies is punctuated by conflicts, big and small – just like anywhere else – but Mennonites have a number of distinctive methods for dealing with them. You can, for example, whisper about them with your spouse late at night in bed and hope he or she doesn't betray you to the elders. Pray for resolution. Ask for guidance from your church pastor, who may also be the source of the conflict. Turn the other cheek, according to the words of Jesus. And, if it's bad enough, freeze out the individual creating the problem until they cease to exist in your thoughts, or even better, have that person shunned. (Shunning happens by order of the elders. It involves a complete denial of the individual's existence. It is a method of conflict avoidance that maintains the righteousness of the community while preventing any resolution or possibility of justice. It is murder without killing and it creates deep-seated wells of rage that find no release.)

War is hell, it's true. *Shouldn't be exposed* is another hell. *Shouldn't be exposed* stifles and silences and violates. *Shouldn't be exposed* refuses and ignores and shames. *Shouldn't be exposed* shields bullies and tyrants. I have seen it in my own life.

When my sister was ten years old, she was grabbed off the street, driven around for a while by a group of teenage boys unknown to her or any of our family, doused in some brown, toxic liquid and dropped back off in front of our home. The white furry hat that she'd just received as a Christmas present was ruined and had to be thrown into the garbage. That's all I know about that. I don't know what else happened in the car. Police weren't called, nobody was called, it had happened and then there was silence and over time it seemed as though it might not have happened after all.

My grandmother, my father's mother, was a secret alcoholic. Our community was dry, drinking was a sin, but she shoplifted bottles of vanilla extract from the local grocer and drank them one by one alone in the darkness of her small apartment. My parents would let themselves in with a key that they kept, pick her up, clean her up and put her to bed. My mother had mentioned to me that she suspected that my grandmother had been assaulted by a group of local men when she was a young woman, but it was never spoken of, never investigated. Every few weeks, the owner of the grocery store where my grandmother stole vanilla would call my father and tell him the sum total of the missing bottles – he never confronted my grandmother directly – and my father would write him a cheque and that was that, until the next time, when the same process would be repeated.

My other grandmother, my mother's mother, was stood up at the altar twice by my grandfather until finally, on the third try, they were married. She had thirteen children, buried six of them as babies and spent a great deal of time praying. She would never even have suggested to my grandfather that his sexual desire was becoming an inconvenience. In fact, it was killing her, each pregnancy posing another threat to her life. At the onset of menopause and with the blessed end of pregnancies clearly in sight, she dropped dead of high blood pressure.

My father had a nervous breakdown at the age of seventeen and was diagnosed with bipolar disorder, then called manic depression. His family never spoke of it except to berate him for being weak and effeminate and not devout enough a Christian, even though he attended church relentlessly, taught Sunday school, prayed his heart out for relief and never missed a sermon.

When I was twelve, the car dealership next door wanted to expand their parking lot and they put pressure on my father to sell our house. My father didn't want to sell the house he had built himself for his new bride and the offspring that followed, and my mother encouraged him to fight, but he didn't once argue or put up any kind of resistance. Business was next to godliness in our town and if my father refused to sell his house and beautiful yard filled with chokecherry trees and Saskatoon trees and petunias and tiger lilies and home-made birdhouses painted with cheerful colours then he truly was a sinner. He sold the house for cheap and mourned his loss quietly. I remember my mother slinging her arm around my father's broad shoulders and whispering, 'Defend yourself, man,' and my father smiling mysteriously, with no words attached.

My mother's cousin received a Rhodes Scholarship to study at the University of Oxford and just a few months into the first term he died there, mysteriously, under suspicious circumstances, or according to God's will, in which case what was there to do about it? His parents chose not to hear any details of an investigation or an autopsy. What if their son had died from a drug overdose, or sexual misadventure, or suicide? If they don't know, then they don't feel obligated to condemn him as a sinner, and they can imagine their bright, young, beloved son in heaven.

My son's girlfriend told me a story about an Italian friend of hers. This Italian friend had an aunt who was absolutely furious with her brother for something they've all since forgotten. In order for her brother to know the extent of her rage she dragged a dead and bloodied deer carcass (I'm not sure where she got it from) onto his driveway for him to discover in the morning. That dead deer carcass said, 'Don't Fuck With Me!' Her brother got the message. He apologized. She made him prove he meant it. He convinced her of his contrition. They laughed. They clinked shot glasses of grappa and drank to peace. *Basta*! Well, I don't know exactly how it all went down but I've been so envious of this Italian brother and sister duo ever since my son's girlfriend told me the story.

During my twenty-year marriage, which ultimately ended in divorce and a tsunami of agony and madness and guilt for thinking that I had destroyed my innocent family out of pure selfishness and conceit, and with the thought that I should probably destroy myself before I could cause more damage, I would sometimes air my complaints to my husband after he'd been drinking and when he was just about to fall asleep. I knew that he wouldn't remember what I had said but at least I would have gotten it off my chest. It was a perfect arrangement. I could speak up but it wouldn't turn into a huge blowout. I would talk about mundane things, mostly, how it bugged me that we always had to have supper at 6 p.m. sharp, for instance, or that he didn't seem enthusiastic about my decision to join the Dakar Desert Rally, but I'd often get into bigger issues too;

fundamental questions about our happiness and our compatibility. He would nod and smile, his eyes closed, and tell me we'd work it all out, he had to sleep, sorry. In the morning he'd have no memory of the conversation. In true Mennonite fashion, I had managed to take the edge off my disappointment and dissatisfaction (by saying a kind of prayer, pretending that someone was listening), without exposing myself, without provoking a big, ugly fight, and without changing a thing.

Between 2005 and 2009, in a very isolated Mennonite colony in Bolivia, 130 women and girls between the ages of three and sixty were raped by what many in the community believed to be ghosts, or Satan, as punishment for their sins. These girls and women were waking up in the morning sore, in pain, and often bleeding. These mysterious attacks went on for years. If the women complained they weren't believed and their stories were chalked up to 'wild female imagination'.

Finally, it was revealed that the women had been telling the truth. Two men from the community were caught in the middle of the night as they were climbing into a neighbour's bedroom window. The men were forced into a confession. They and seven other locals would spray an animal anaesthetic created by a local veterinarian through the screen windows of a house, knocking unconscious all occupants. They would climb in, rape the victims, and get out.

These Mennonite colonies are self-policed, except in cases of murder. The bishop and the elders came up with a solution to the problem of how to punish the offenders. They locked all nine men into sheds and basements, and the idea was that they would stay there for decades. Also, they would instruct these men to ask for forgiveness from the women. If the women refused to forgive these men then God would not forgive the women. If the women did not accept the men's apology they would have to leave the colony for the outside world, of which they knew nothing.

Eventually, this outside world was made aware of the Mennonite 'ghost rapes' and the perpetrators were arrested by the Bolivian police and put on trial by the Bolivian criminal court. According to sources within the community, the rapes have continued and no offers of counselling have been accepted by the elders on behalf of the women and girls. One explanation they made for refusing help was that, because the victims were sedated during the attacks, they couldn't possibly be suffering from psychological trauma.

Abe Warkentin, founder of *Die Mennonitische Poste*, the most widely read Mennonite newspaper across North and South America and whose headquarters are located in my home town, has called the Mennonites 'a broken people'. He has said that in our communities there continues to resound a 'deafening silence' when it comes to these crimes and issues, and he describes the scandal as 'little more than an enlargement of social problems, in which more energy is put into hiding them than confronting and solving them'.

M y father, after politely inquiring as to when the next freight train was scheduled to pass through the tiny village he had walked to, killed himself by kneeling in front of it. Blank pieces of paper were found scattered next to his body. My sister killed herself twelve years later in an identical fashion. Earlier she had left a note that listed the many people she had loved and had added a plea for forgiveness and the hope that God would accept her into His kingdom. When I was a teenager my sister put her hands on my shoulders, as though knighting me, and told me that I was a 'survivor'. What does that mean? What does that require?

In 2008, I met Rudy Wiebe for the first time. A book tour had been arranged for the two of us in Germany. We would travel together from one small Mennonite village to the next, reading from our work and answering questions from audiences. A tall long-haired Lithuanian Mennonite living in Bonn drove us around from colony to colony and acted as our cultural attaché. He and Rudy Wiebe sat in the front seat of the car and told each other hilarious stories in Plautdietsch, the unwritten language of the Mennonites, and I sat in the back seat amazed that I was on a book tour with the guy who everybody had whispered about – the myth himself!

Rudy Wiebe was the same age my father would have been. They had a similar body type: tall, slightly stooped. He was formal and polite, like my father, with a way of looking up at things suddenly from a bowed head, so that in that instant, when he looked up or at you, his eyes were wide and his forehead was creased. He was a sort of folk hero in these communities, no longer condemned as a renegade traitor but sweetly embraced by these conservative Mennonites as a famous writer they could call their own, a prodigal son who spoke their language and who was no longer as harsh a critic of their culture as he'd been in his youth.

Rudy and I spent a week together on the road and had come to our last event in a tiny Mennonite town whose name I can't remember. Once again, the audience was overjoyed to hear Rudy speak and mostly puzzled or just indifferent when it was my turn. I don't speak Plautdietsch so a translator had to help me out when there were questions from the audience. I was reading from my novel, *A Complicated Kindness*, which is about a sixteen-year-old girl whose Mennonite family is torn apart by fundamentalism. My reading didn't leave a great taste in the mouths of these German Mennonites. Afterwards, an angry-looking woman stood up and asked to be given the microphone. Her question was directed at me. It went on for a long time, in Plautdietsch, and when she was finished the translator faltered, a bit reluctant to tell me what the woman had said. Rudy Wiebe had understood it all and was busy making notes on a pad of paper. The translator told me that the woman had said my book was filthy and that my characters' mockery of Menno Simons, the man who started the Mennonites in Holland five hundred years ago, was sacrilegious and sinful. She said that if she had a sixteen-year-old daughter she would not allow her to read my book. As the translator translated I smiled and nodded politely. When he was finished I thanked the woman for her comments. I was at a loss as to what to say next. Rudy Wiebe motioned for me to hand over the microphone.

He walked to the edge of the stage and spoke directly to this woman in her language. After a minute or two, the woman stormed out of the room, dragging her mortified husband along with her. Rudy continued to talk for a while and then handed the microphone to the translator who translated everything back into English for me and the few other English speakers in the room.

Rudy had defended me. He had told this woman, 'No. You're wrong.' He said that the reaction to my book had reminded him of the Mennonite reaction to his first novel, *Peace Shall Destroy Many*. He told the people in the room that however they might feel about the swearing in the book, it was at least an honest book, and that the conversations it had generated were important ones and that it, in its way, was advocating for necessary change within our culture; it was holding us accountable as Mennonites to our humanity, our humanness; it was asking us to be self-critical, to accept reality, and to love better. He may have said other things that weren't translated, I don't know.

What I'll remember is that on that day Rudy Wiebe stood up in front of a Mennonite 'congregation' and fought for me. My father would have approved. He may not have been able to do it himself but I know he would have appreciated the scene, this long-ago subversive hero defending his very own daughter.

Rudy and I took a train to Frankfurt the next day, where we were catching different flights home to Canada. The train was packed and, with the exception of one seat, there was standing room only. Rudy gestured for me to take the seat, but I hesitated. He looked tired and I knew the week had been hard on him. Again he reminded me of my father before he died, smiling valiantly, sadness in his eyes. I shook my head and gestured for him to take the seat. I was happy to stand, no problem. The train was moving fast and things, life, on the outside became a blur. I watched him as he gazed through the window out at the German countryside, pensive. Soon he was asleep and the train ticket he held in his hand slipped from his fingers and fell to the floor. ∎

Matilda Gustavsson at 15, from her school yearbook, 2002
Courtesy of the author

THE SUFFERINGS OF THIS PRESENT TIME ARE NOT WORTHY TO BE COMPARED WITH THE GLORY WHICH SHALL BE REVEALED IN US

Matilda Gustavsson

TRANSLATED FROM THE SWEDISH BY PETER GRAVES

A bruised reed shall he not break, and the smoking flax shall he not quench.

Markus's leg grew longer on New Year's Day. His left leg was a couple of inches shorter than his right and it grew before our eyes, though my eyes happened to have been closed. His whole leg: bones, skin, the hard muscles in his calves that I didn't want to touch.

I still didn't believe it. I was on the point of getting up and walking out. Until the other thing happened.

His name is Markus and he's almost twenty years old. He's my leader.

The high school, a rust-coloured brick building on the outskirts of Markaryd, is closed for the Christmas holidays and we have taken it over – a hundred young Christians from all over Sweden. It's a New Year camp and it's the morning of New Year's Day. I see him in the corridor. I see him from behind – his shoulders, and those strong thighs moving in his torn white jeans. I walk a little faster and have almost caught up with him when he sees me and smiles.

'Happy New Year!'

He is shorter than me. I would like the two of us to have a conversation, just the two of us, about anything at all. But I can never think of what to say. Then the others turn up. Markus unlocks the group room and switches on the flickering strip light. There are stacks of chairs in the corners of the room and on one wall there is an anatomical chart of Swedish farm animals. The only window is above us: a square of soft grey in the ceiling.

The camp is divided into small groups, five people in each. We come from different towns, so we don't know each other. We sit on the floor in a circle. We are ill at ease, but we have our faith in common and that is what truly matters. There is a girl with dark hair who smiles a lot and doesn't hide the zigzag scars on her arms; another is a new convert. There is a boy who attends a handball academy and there is Jakob, who is fifteen though I'd have guessed he was twelve. The chain around his neck looks hip-hop.

It's a relief when Markus breaks the silence because his voice provides focus. He says the Holy Spirit has spoken and told him that one of the members of our group is longing for the gift of grace. Has any of us had a sense of that?

'I have.' Jakob speaks. He hasn't said a word until then. He sounds terrified. 'I have.' But as soon as the words are out, his face goes blank. He has thrown himself open and suddenly he can see the rest of us in the group.

Markus tells us that his legs are different lengths. He gets a sore back when he takes any exercise and the doctors say the pain will get worse with time. He sits down on the floor with his back against the wall and stretches out his legs for us to see. His left foot does not reach as far as his right foot and we immediately have a pretty good idea of what we have to do.

Without making eye contact with one another we gather around and place our hands on his body, on his head, on his arms and on his back while Jakob takes hold of Markus's leg. We form a clumsy phalanx of sorts.

I mumble, 'Jesus, may Thy will be done,' and try to concentrate, but Markus's ankles are showing between his socks and the frayed legs of his jeans and somehow that glimpse of flesh seems so naked. It's so ordinary, unlike the handball player's chest or the girl's scarred arms. She is pressing her hand on Jakob, who is squeezing Markus's leg.

Will the bones creak as they grow?

In a moment of clarity I realise for the first time in my life that I do not believe. It is not going to happen, it simply *cannot* happen. When we finally give up, how are we going to be able to look one another in the eye without embarrassment? If I lose my faith and stray from the straight path, where will I end up? There is both darkness and a secret longing in that question: a little green light. A jubilant exit sign. Out of here.

I look up at the grey clouds and I know that there are other cities beneath the heavens. Great cities. Cities bursting with music and magazines about people who matter and things that are visible. I shut my eyes and the skylight becomes a bright square.

I do not believe.

A sound, a bright cry, brings me back to earth.

Jakob is sitting there staring at his trembling hands. His sobs are uneven. He is saying 'L-Lord G-God'. Tears are pouring from the handball player's eyes and he leans against the wall, hiding his face. The girl with the scars is smiling and the new convert is laughing: 'I *saw*,' she says, pointing her finger at him like a child.

My eyes had been closed but it's quite obvious now. Markus's left leg is exactly the same length as his right leg. He stands up and stretches his body and his arms up towards the ceiling.

And I still don't believe.

I am on the point of getting up and leaving. This is where the story should end, but it doesn't.

When a group of us stood in a circle outside the Central Station two days before New Year's Eve the temperature was minus sixteen. The cold felt like small knives pricking our skin. That early in the morning the place was completely deserted.

We lived farthest east so we were the first to be picked up. We were a new generation and we were on our way to the New Year camp at Markaryd. Emma, my best friend, was sitting next to me.

Alexander was sitting with the generation born in '85.

The back of his neck and his buzz cut poked up above the back of the seat.

Small towns, pickup stops. We checked them out as they climbed aboard. A guy with curly hair produced a guitar and we all sang into the darkness outside. There were grey streaks of dawn out there. Alexander and the others raised their hands. A few people spoke in tongues.

I thought of all the cars that passed our brightly lit silver bus. They must have wondered who we were.

Once, much later, I referred to us as religious teenyboppers, but that was only true in the beginning. For some years my teenage Christian group Agape – which means 'love' in Swedish – had become more and more radical. As many people as possible had to be saved in time for the advent of eternity. *For we wrestle not against flesh and blood, but against principalities, against powers, against the rulers of the darkness of this world.*

The autumn, winter and first spring were pure exhilaration, as if we were conquering not just the city but the whole universe. We owned the truth about why we were here and where we were going, which was an apocalypse bigger than all the war and exultation the world had known. It felt as if we were expanding, becoming important, becoming great.

It would be a good few years before I was able to articulate the reality. That we were shrinking. That all of us singing along on that silver bus were on our way to becoming so small.

Alexander stood up every so often and shouted to a gang sitting at the back. Usually it was a joke, in which case he would stay on his feet for a while to receive their laughter. He always wore the same jeans and T-shirt, as if he woke up in the morning and simply marched straight out. He was the one of us who would go farthest, so far that he even renounced his body.

A lexander and his sister had moved to our city the summer before the New Year camp, but I had already heard of them. Alexander had apparently left the Church for a time and done a lot of partying.

Some of the 85-ers who had been leaders at various Christian camps said that the two siblings questioned everything. In the middle of an instructional session they might come up with a question to which the speaker had no answer. And everyone had heard the story of the sick trick that had been hatched during a four-week summer camp. It had been Alexander's idea and started with the camp participants being told that one of them was living under threat, with a secret identity. Then the leaders pushed it a stage further. An unknown car appeared in the vicinity of the camp and a figure was seen in the woods. They hired a masked man with a chainsaw, who had terrified some of the campers so much that they hadn't been able to sleep for days. But the sickest part of the whole thing was when one of the campers – a fourteen-year-old – had gone up to the masked man, raised his hands to the heavens and said that if the others were allowed to live, he was ready: 'I am ready to go home.'

Emma and I and some of the others were gathered around the 85-er who was telling the story. She had been there.

We laughed at the story, but not at its conclusion.

He had offered his life.

A gape, our group, met every Friday in the House, a chapel in the middle of the city. Whenever there was a disco in the dining hall at my school, everyone else in my class went – everyone except me and the Muslim boy, whose dad was manifestly crazy. I soon discovered that other people considered my faith to be strange, especially the people who wrote in the magazines I had started reading in the library. But that just made it all the more precious.

The sky outside the House was always the same on Sundays, the colour of porridge or milk. There was a cross hanging on an invisible cord at the front of the chapel, a reminder of Our Lord God, who chose to become a little human being and to pay for our sins with His blood. We believed in the Father, the Son and the Holy Spirit, but we talked mostly about Jesus: He was the first of the three and He was the one I used to pray to.

We sat in rows during the service: children of the House who had fallen in love and were bearing new children in their swollen bellies; the fellow who had stopped drinking; unmarried people. People who came and went. Our parents. The woman surrounded by voices no one else could hear: sometimes she would answer them, sometimes she would tell them to shut up, sometimes she would tell us what they were saying. There was always someone prepared to listen.

The songs we sang had many verses. They told of our inner struggles and the short span of our time on this earth: *It's but a twilight hour I dwell on earth.* The saddest tunes made me shudder. And with the same depth of feeling we sang of hope, of meeting again beyond the grave when all the tears would be wiped from our eyes.

The sublimity drew me in.

It calmed the disquiet within me.

The lectern in the House was grey. My father would stand there with his leather Bible when he wasn't off speaking at chapels in other towns. When he was away I made him promise to be home by a certain time and as the kitchen clock approached the stated hour I would wander blindly around our house. Only when I heard the car door slam in the street would my eyes begin to see colours again.

Dad and I often talked about faith. He would listen to me for hours, listening as if he was ready to change his mind at any moment, though he never actually did. When I learned about feminism I yelled at him that the House was pitiful and that I was more intelligent than the men who had the right to preach. He smiled and said that he agreed with that last point – the one about who was brightest. He was a sixth-form physics teacher and he used to say that when it came to the crunch, the natural sciences didn't have all the answers. He often said it, sometimes in quite lofty terms: 'A human being is more than atoms and chemical processes.'

My grandfather had been the preacher before him. Old people looked at me in an impressed sort of way when they realised I was his granddaughter. When I was little I had the feeling of having been chosen. I was a girl and the eldest child, like Princess Victoria, but with a more onerous birthright, because we knew that Jesus was the only road to heaven and the only road that did not lead to hell.

The pain my family suffered much later came from that conviction and the fact that we loved one another. It was the dark logic of love. Which is why it really shook me that they didn't do more to stop me, that they didn't cling on to my legs. That they let me go.

Teenage years were supposed to be wonderful years. You were supposed to make friends for life and perhaps even meet your husband. It was a decisive time in that you either stood firm in your faith or you slipped away.

I had occasionally sat up late in the kitchen with Mum and Grandma and heard, for instance, about the people who had gone abroad and fallen blindly in love. Things had turned out as they had turned out. These stories had me clutching the arm of the chair – or anything else I could cling to – in order to prevent myself from leaving.

Soon I would start attending Agape meetings and going to camp. There were brochures in the House with pictures of water fights and girls riding piggyback.

I reached thirteen and my anxiety began to turn into something that didn't have a name. A dizzying panic. I began to see everything from outside obsessively – myself, the faces of others, the Agape hierarchy and how lost I was in it. Coming together in the hall provided temporary freedom in that we sat motionless in rows and it was possible to disappear into the crowd and let your voice merge with the others through verse after verse. And just gaze at the lighted candles.

I turned fourteen and my panic became more and more threatening. I prayed to Jesus and the feeling disappeared. I was overjoyed. But it returned just a few days later, and again a couple of weeks after that. It would never stop coming back.

The first time I saw Alexander was in September, the autumn I was starting Year Nine, the autumn before the New Year camp. I was on my way to the House and Agape with throbbing fingers and dyed blonde hair. Two girls carrying bottles passed me. I wondered where they were going. Music was spilling out from other buildings, 'When We Were Winning' and other songs.

One of the boys was standing right at the front with his guitar. We had recently started singing new tunes, songs of praise that were projected as overheads onto the wall behind the cross. The songs allowed for brighter feelings and the words dealt with being touched by Thee and sacrificing everything for Thy sake.

There were already several people in the queue when Emma and I went through to the refreshment room. Your place in the queue decided which dining table you would sit at and who you would be sitting opposite. That's when we saw them.

Alexander and his sister were bent forward over a bowl of what looked like meringue and ice cream and we noticed them because they were moving. That was the remarkable thing about them: even when they were standing still they seemed to be laughing and weeping, about to rush off. Intuitively I had a mental picture of them as children: phenomenally strong, fighting.

Afterwards we talked about them all the time. I talked about Alexander, Emma about his sister. They were short and broad-shouldered. They had the same narrow feline eyes and rubbery mouths. But her hips made her bow legs more noticeable than his. Small fair hairs on Alexander's strong arms: it was impossible to imagine that one day he would starve himself. It was the beginning of September and he was pouring cream – white and viscous – over the meringue and ice cream.

During evening prayers we used tea lights to brighten the darkness in the hall. We were sitting down singing as usual when his sister stood up. She raised her hands high above her head, higher than all of us. A moment later one of the 85-ers from the House rose to his feet. His movements looked awkward but happy; he was like a calf. Emma and I were sitting behind him.

Then Alexander got up and said that he used to be religious on Sundays; Christian out of habit. But that was before he had been transformed by the Holy Spirit, he said, speaking without notes. *I would thou wert cold or hot. So then because thou art lukewarm, and neither hot nor cold, I will spue thee out of my mouth.* He leafed through the Book of Revelation, fingers fumbling, and I wanted to hold him, to put his neck, his arms, his legs in a lock. Alexander asked whether we were serious about everything we preached in the House. And if so, why couldn't we be Christians unreservedly? How could we be lukewarm?

The Holy Spirit began to emerge in Agape during the autumn before the New Year camp. It became virtually separate from the Trinity. The Spirit was simultaneously both a being in its own right and God's power. Unlike Jesus, the Holy Spirit had no lines of its own in the Bible. There were no safe words you could copy out on a slip of paper and carry in your jacket pocket: it revealed itself as flames of fire on the heads of the disciples or as a strange tongue. It was a personal clap of thunder and only to be understood by meeting it every day. *Good Morning, Holy Spirit.* Many of us read that book by Benny Hinn.

The emphasis on the Holy Spirit was a new dimension, a feeling that anything might happen.

And this change was accompanied by increasing fervour. Before this we had hardly given one another more than a hug when we said goodbye, but now I saw hands stroking backs, I saw tears being shed and bones stretched to their proper length. The music got louder and the warmth kindled within the circle created an icy chill outside. I had always wept before Jesus, but not in front of other people.

I sat motionless on my chair.

The Holy Spirit did not touch me. I was like air before it. Emma went to receive intercession from his sister and I saw their fair and dark hair mingle, saw his sister's hand on Emma's thigh and the tips of their fingers brushing.

Alexander was sitting with his head bowed and something monstrous heaving within him, through his shoulders and over his lips.

I knew what it was, though I had never seen it. No one spoke in tongues in the House.

Alexander was conscious of that boundary and it looked as though he was struggling with himself and biting his tongue, but he was unable to resist and it came. Like Russian or Dutch. I saw him gagging, nauseous.

In the beginning of December I ventured to raise a hand as we sang our songs of praise. Stiffly, as if my arm was prosthetic, I stretched it a little higher. I meant it.

What was happening in Agape changed me. It had to do with my sense of how we must look to other people. I had a feeling that anyone who spoke in tongues must be sick, that anyone who lived just for eternity was dangerous. It drove my faith onwards, towards life at its extreme. When we raised our hands every Friday night we were either raising them towards empty space or it was serious.

If every word in the Bible were true, if God existed, if He saw me and saw the whole world, then His gaze transformed everything. It could recast the rows of houses and the black fields that surrounded our terraced estate. It was larger than the crow trees and the road to school, larger than the footsteps in the corridor and my dizzying panic.

If everything that the House and Dad believed were true, how could we just sit there in motionless rows? *If* was a colour on a palette very different to the pale milkiness of Sunday.

That's why I said that stuff about drugs. Before Christmas it was my turn to open the meeting at Agape. Previously it had always been enough to just say hello and welcome, but we were now expected to stir the others, to arouse something in them. I read out one of my favourite passages from the Bible: *For I reckon that the sufferings of this present time are not worthy to be compared with the glory which shall be revealed in us.*

And in a quiet voice I said that if we have an eternity before us there is no need for us to become stressed about success and the like. We had no need to become popular. I was looking down at my paper the whole time: 'We do not need to experiment with drugs. We don't need to worry about *carpe diem*.'

I had been polishing the expression all night and it made them smile. Alexander said 'Amen!' My words had struck something within him.

I felt a rush of strength. Wanted to say it again.

'I'd really like to have that *carpe diem* bit embroidered on a wall hanging,' he said to me later in the queue for refreshments.

His feline eyes were close, narrowed, promising.

'I can ask my grandmother,' I said.

What an answer!

But he was no longer thinking of me and later, during evening prayers, he rose to his feet and said that the Holy Spirit had spoken to him about eternity.

'Like, heaven is obviously fantastic, but we can't just sit here and yearn to be there,' Alexander said.

God had great plans for us here and now. If we were His children, we were also His heirs. The power and the glory belonged to us.

'Many of the people in the House believe that life is all about marrying young, going to church and having a nine-to-five job, but that's not exactly how the apostles lived,' he said.

The chill returned. It was not possible to turn invisible when we sang the new songs, and speaking in tongues was spreading in a hierarchical way: the first people to receive the gift were Alexander's friends. They spoke quietly and covered their faces with their arms so as not to disturb the rest of us. If the Holy Spirit was freedom, why did they all look the same when they were seized by it?

I rang Dad. He came and we walked down the street to the car. In the past our parents had always collected us at eleven o'clock, but the songs of praise now went on forever and I had no idea what time it was. There were Christmas displays everywhere. The town was full of bright red lamps and the hum of electricity, but the celebrations had quietened down and there was no bass thump. We were soon going to be off to a completely new sort of New Year camp and Dad said he was glad that Agape seemed to have become so fervent.

In Markaryd Emma and I inflated our airbeds on the floor of one of the classrooms before going off to different groups.

Sitting in a circle we said our names. My leader was called Markus and before we broke up he said that the Holy Spirit was going to work in our group and that we should have high expectations.

For study purposes the camp divided up into workshops.

I had chosen 'The Last Time', the other 87-ers from the House had gone for 'The Gifts of the Spirit'. When we met afterwards it was obvious that something had happened. You could see their swollen eyes from the other end of the corridor. The boys had been crying. They said it was difficult to put into words what had happened. It was the Holy Spirit.

'Those of us who wanted the gift of tongues were to go forward, and then it happened. It came.'

'I didn't expect it, but it *happened*.'

'It wasn't like anything you can imagine.'

I drew Emma aside, but before I had time to say anything she told me that she, too, had received the gift of tongues. Several weeks earlier. Not out at the front of a stage when emotions were running high, but one day after school when she was alone in her room. It had been so private that she hadn't told anyone, apart from Alexander's sister.

The old year came to an end. Wrapped up in warm clothes we all gathered in the schoolyard waiting for the stroke of twelve. My ugly green down jacket. Lighted candles were handed out. A number of us carried flaming torches as we processed through the town singing the new songs. Some people were crying. I saw Alexander. I always saw him, in spite of the fact that everyone knew there was no chance of him ever becoming part of an item. His calling was a greater one. I never fantasised about becoming his girlfriend, just that he might simply do a complete turnaround and give up eternity for me. Emma and I walked in silence. We encountered families who waved or pointed, and we walked past windows and parties. 'When We Were Winning'. We met dark-eyed drunken teenagers on holiday from the red-brick school. They joined us and tried to get us to have a beer.

I felt the triumph of the martyr. I felt shame.

What if I were to choose a different path, to fall away? But where to? An exit was simply unthinkable.

Happy New Year.

A dark sky hangs over the morning of New Year's Day. The clouds were heavy with old seawater and probably with all the tears shed during the night. Emma and I walk across the schoolyard with the others. The dining room has just opened and the queue is not moving even though everyone is in motion – stamping their feet on the spot. Alexander is standing with a cluster of people and when he glances my way I try to look preoccupied, as if I'm having a conversation or listening to a joke. I stare fixedly at anyone. Emma only has eyes for his sister. The breakfast queue is motionless, while the greatest thing that has ever happened to me is coming closer. And it is not the business of the leg.

M arkus's left leg is exactly the same length as his right leg. In spite of which I still do not believe.

I have a slight feeling he may have faked it, but what I see for the most part is the way the others react: I see the tears, the giggles, the handball guy who has started walking round and round in a foolish circle.

I am just about to get up and leave the room when the other thing happens. It's difficult to reconstruct it afterwards because it just happens. It comes over me – a sensation. My skin becomes all ants, so that the boundaries and contours of my being simultaneously dissolve and are 100 per cent crystal clear. I exist.

Just like the dizzying panic, but in reverse: an ecstatic fall.

When I start coming back down to earth, my face is on the floor by a puddle of salt tears. I am convinced that God is in our group room. He has performed a miracle.

He is here and this dizzy feeling is like the anxiety you feel when you are in love: the moment when the body recognises what the head knows, that the other person is independent, that he will be just as real and alive if you die, or after the door has closed behind you. A mystery that can simply turn away and leave.

That's how I feel for a few seconds before the question of who God is takes form. When so many people are suffering why would He choose to make a healthy leg a couple of inches longer?

And what is reality now?

Reality is such that a part of the body can grow longer at any time. Reality is such that death is not the end. I will exist forever. We will never ever cease to be. Not even if we want to, not even if we leap off a precipice. And if we are going to live for all eternity there can be nothing more important than bearing witness to the one and only path. In the face of that reality I see before me the girl in the House, the one surrounded by voices no one else can hear. I remember the time when, as a child, I saw a UFO in the sky: for a few petrifying moments, until Dad managed to convince me it was a satellite, I was filled with a horror I'd never known before. People would not believe me. No one would believe what I'd seen. I would feature as a sad figure in some TV documentary and I would end up being the sole bearer of the truth. Year after year.

There is no way back in Markaryd. Not for the five of us who have seen a leg grow longer.

I lie down on my back and the skylight in the roof becomes

a square of loneliness that grows bigger and bigger. It takes over the whole of the room. I see the anatomical wallchart of Swedish farm animals and I see Jakob who is still sitting on his hands. I see the dusty stacked chairs and the door. More clearly than ever I see the cities and my secret yearning to get away. I will never be able to deny what has happened. I will remain here forever.

A little while later I am standing in the bathroom, looking at the black mascara under my eyes. I wash away my fear with ice-cold water and a quick look of wonder passes across my face: hubris.

In a world of suffering why would God choose to make a leg grow a few inches longer?

Why, after always remaining silent when I have called upon Him about disease and death, would He suddenly give me a *feeling*?

In that moment I experience the very emptiness of the event as an overpowering and warm sign. As love, generous in its abundance. He stopped. He saw. He saw *me*.

The evening of New Year's Day is the last evening in the camp and rain fills the potholes in the tarmac. We gather to sing songs of praise in the main school hall and I see Jakob in one of the middle aisles, a flapping movement in the corner of my eye. He raises his arms and jumps up and down in his big sweater. Speaking into a microphone, someone commands the Devil to release his hold on our tongues and the hall fills with strange languages.

I've told Emma about the leg and about my feeling, and then I told her I had 'received the gift of tongues'. I made a slightly more lucid story of the experience and I believe it. I test it out during the meeting. The words come.

It sounds like Russian or Dutch and I've asked myself a thousand times since then where the borderline runs between what is truly great and what is simple group psychology. Between the genuine experience and the faked.

I do recognise, however, that it's an impossible distinction to make, that even in the most pregnant of dramas there is something naked, a raw point. Lights sweep across the hall, the music gets louder and drowns out everything, the drums beat in time with a hundred pounding hearts from all over Sweden. And it's only afterwards that you ask yourself the question about true or false. But when you are part of that sensation – the feeling of something larger than life – no such borderlines exist.

I would reach that point again later: the moment when I almost went under the wheels of a lorry and was sure I was going to die, but lived; or when I was with him – not Alexander. Someone else. Those occasions were, perhaps, just as overpowering, but they weren't the first.

When we meet for the last time the members of the group give one another long hugs. There is a new brightness in Jakob's eyes. Markus comes walking along the corridor and when he sees us he performs a jokey little skip for joy. Two legs of exactly the same length and heels that meet.

We sit in a circle on the floor and Markus exhorts us to seek even more gifts. He talks of prophecy, saying that God has messages for us before we leave for home. He says we must be truly watchful, for the Holy Spirit can speak within us. Like demons. I close my eyes and observe how thoughts and images criss-cross my eyelids, like messengers. As if I am a white screen. Who is the sender?

All of a sudden Jakob says that an image has come to him. He is seeing a red shed, a woodshed perhaps, with a child's bike outside. I listen devoutly and I say, 'That might be our summer cottage.'

Writing this piece many years later I remember what my dad used to say about the natural sciences not being able to explain everything and that a human being is more than atoms and chemical processes. I realise that the five of us shrank to something that was even smaller.

Within the group, that sense of smallness is something wonderful, a kind of gentle capitulation. I am part of someone else's plan. I have discarded myself. I turn to Jakob: 'What else do you see?'

During the years that followed many of those involved in Agape would talk with conviction of being guided by the Spirit – the countries to be visited after leaving school, the money that was suddenly in their bank accounts, the delayed trains and unexpected meetings. Often it depended on the exact minute. And the years passed. It was like a new and paradoxical time in which life was eternal and every second important, like gazing up, eyes wide in wonder – that, no doubt, is why so many later grew weary.

The lost generation of the House, my father said.

Emma and I were the youngest. We were not present at the meetings at which Dad pleaded with the Agape committee. The adults were concerned that our spirituality had gone too far and that we were preaching the kind of progress associated with the Word of Life movement.

Not even Alexander had been to its seminary in Uppsala, though we sometimes watched videos of the meetings there and saw honey-coloured light flooding a high stage on which the speakers were as well turned out as celebrities in a magazine. Nothing could have been less like the House and less like Alexander.

I still think about the mystery he was, how he always talked of victory but then took the hard path.

He could have travelled around the world as some rich evangelists do. He could have changed direction, taking over a company or a nightclub empire, conquering the great cities. But he didn't.

After working as a missionary in a small village for many years he stopped eating. He did so in order to get closer to God, and in the end his body simply collapsed. How do you explain that to hospital staff in Sweden? How do you talk about a love affair with something intangible?

We step down from the silver bus and Dad comes to meet me in his blue anorak. When we are in the car, before he starts the engine, I tell him about the leg and about the gift of tongues. The words I use are not really up to the task and they sound just like everyone else's: I didn't expect it, but it *did happen*.

Dad listens. He seems doubtful about the leg that grew longer. It is dangerous to turn God into a performance, he says, but he does believe in the feeling I had.

'That kind of experience of God is something I've only ever been able to dream of.'

All sins and blasphemies will be forgiven for the sons of men. But he that shall blaspheme against the Holy Ghost hath never forgiveness, but is in danger of eternal damnation.

Ten years later I meet Markus again. I am twenty-five and living in Malmö. I am not living in 'the Last Time' but in a stream of weeks, months and days I rarely manage to keep up with. I am afraid of death. I never talk about the leg, not even when I'm drunk, even though the story is so strange, and even though now you can see legs that grow longer on YouTube. At that New Year camp I had a transcendent experience that I found impossible to explain and there was no way I could separate it from the context of healing.

Markus is crossing the street and I recognise his profile and his dark hair. And at the very same moment my body remembers, too, and another perception is activated. I am back in the parallel reality of our group room in Markaryd, where we wept and held on to one another.

So I hurry to catch up with him. Dig my nails into his shoulder.

He looks at me, fear in his brown eyes, but then he recognises me.

'How's your leg?'

'Aha, indeed. That New Year. That really was something,' he says, smiling politely at the memory.

I repeat my question. 'How's the leg?'

'The fantastic thing is that the Holy Spirit made it grow longer on a later occasion too. He wanted to use me again.'

For the rest of our short conversation I'm at a loss for words. They are just too small.

I don't manage to formulate a single question, apart from the obvious one.

'So your leg became shorter again then?'

'It isn't unusual. He wants to demonstrate His power to more people,' Markus says in an adult voice.

I stand staring at his solid body. I look down at his two short legs that are of equal length. I check out his calves and his well-exercised thighs, his black Acne jeans.

I've never come across anything so contemptible.

Or such a shabby image of God.

And Jakob? The thin fellow who was given the gift of healing and laid his hands on you?

Markus does not know what has become of Jakob. Doesn't know his surname. As for himself, he's just had another child. Another daughter. They attend a wonderfully lively congregation in the city. I can't think of anything to say and he gives me a gentle smile before turning to go. 'I wish you all the very best,' he says. ■

THE SHEPHERDS

Lauren Hough

'Do you remember me?' she asks, as a hopeful smile spreads on her face, like she's trying to tease the right answer out of me. We're not children anymore. We've left. Some of us left with our families, some with our friends and some alone. Now we're living in this other world where we keep having to explain – why we lived in so many countries, why our accents change when we talk to strangers, why we didn't go to school, why we can't sleep. But to one another, to those of us who grew up like me in the Family, we don't have to explain.

Yet on message boards, on Facebook, and now, outside a coffee shop on South Congress in Austin, this same question – 'Do you remember me?' – comes up over and over. It's usually followed by the volley of questions we've tested to figure out who we were then. 'What was your name? Who were your parents? Were you in Osaka? Switzerland?'

Part of the problem with growing up in something so secluded as a cult is that our pasts are so unbelievable we need a witness for our own memory. And so we seek out those who remember.

When I met Ruthie, I was crossing the country in a tiny Winnebago because this is the sort of brilliant idea you get when you can't sleep. My trip stalled in Austin with a broken clutch, so I sent out a message on a board for cult babies, 'Anyone here?'

Ruthie responded and I invited her for coffee. I didn't need to figure out who this woman was, I knew. She was a frazzled German with an American accent who clutched her coffee, her fingers worn ragged. Those calluses and scars were a by-product of what our parents would call 'homeschooling', but whose curriculum was heavy on diaper-changing, cooking and the words of our prophet. With its lack of anything that might be considered a real education, some of us have difficulty finding work that doesn't make our hands bleed.

We were thirteen the last time Ruthie and I saw each other. Her name was Faithy back then and I wasn't allowed to talk to her. In fact, I wasn't allowed to talk to anyone, because the last time I saw her we were both still in the Family and we were in serious trouble.

We lived in a huge, ten-bedroom chalet in Switzerland which had once been a quaint bed and breakfast. If it weren't for the Family's avoidance of even basic upkeep, it would have been like something you'd see on a postcard. Our window boxes were filled with rotting memories of carnations, the roof leaked and the floors sagged under the weight of all the people they supported. We'd managed to cram nearly seventy of us into this particular home. Its one virtue was that it was close enough to the American military bases in Germany that we could pick up Armed Forces Radio. That was important, because I had a radio.

One night, a home shepherd called Auntie Mercy shook my shoulder to wake me. My first thought was that the Romans were at the door. Romans were cops and we practiced constantly for when they made their inevitable raid on our home. As Auntie Mercy put a finger to her lips to shush me, I looked around and saw that the other kids were still asleep. This was not a good sign. I followed her out onto the landing in my undershirt and panties because when a home shepherd summons you, you don't stop to get dressed. She didn't say a word, only turned, and I followed her down the stairs.

The other home shepherds were in the dining room along with the shepherd for my age group, Uncle Stephan, who waved his weirdly hairless arm at me and said, 'Have a seat, sweetie.' When a word like

THE SHEPHERDS

sweetie, so innocent and saccharine, slips out of the wrong mouth, you'll wish you were wearing pants. I sat in the chair facing them, and rubbed my eyes, acting sleepy to buy time, like staring down a gun and pleading for a cigarette.

'Should we pray?' asked Auntie Mercy. We held hands, mine clammy, and we prayed as I flicked a hardened, yellow grain of over-boiled rice with my toe. The eels began to turn in my stomach as I waited for the inevitable next line.

'Do you have anything to tell us?'

I started small with the confessions. I'd played this game before. 'I haven't been putting my heart into my chores,' I said. If I got it right on the first guess, they'd just keep digging for more. I would give them anything. I would have to. But I wasn't giving up my radio.

One thing most cults have in common is you have to give up everything to join. In that home, and every other home I'd lived in, there was a pile somewhere of random items someone had given up to follow Jesus. If Grandma or Aunt Nancy sends you a package, that goes in the pile too. Occasionally, all this crap is divvied out to those who need the supplies, or those with enough pull to get something they want. When I had been tasked to clean up the pile, I found the radio.

Faithy caught me listening the first night. She slept below me, in the middle bunk of the triple-decker. I was up top. Wherever we went, the bunks were built out of two-by-fours and plywood. The mattresses were bare foam, but weren't too bad. The foam was easy to cut into if you wanted to hide something – hard-boiled eggs, a book, a corner of a chocolate bar, or even a radio. Faithy and I hadn't talked much because I had been on silence restriction and not allowed to speak to anyone but a shepherd.

Silence restriction and sign-wearing were the newest tactics in arbitrarily inflicted punishment. Silence restriction is pretty simple to understand. Then we wore signs around our necks made of cardboard or plywood with catchy slogans like SILENCE RESTRICTION or I NEED TO COUNT MY BLESSINGS or PLEASE REMIND ME TO SMILE – that last was being worn by an eight-year-old whose desire to smile

45

remained unchanged. Punishments came and went like any other fad in the outside world but favorite methods included writing essays, memorizing chapters of the Bible, a paper-clip daisy chain wrapped around your head and then hooked to each cheek to force a smile, running laps around a driveway, pointless manual labor, isolation, public beatings, bread-and-water diets. These, usually in some combination, could last days or months and there was no way to tell which way it would go.

Faithy was new to our home, louder than the rest of us had learned to be, and she had more than one pair of socks, a sign she'd been living in smaller homes where kids get things like socks. I met her the night I accidentally pulled out the headphone cord from the radio and she heard the static from the little built-in speaker. From that night on, when we were pretty sure no one else would check on us, she'd climb into my bunk. I snapped the plastic band attaching the earpieces, we'd each take one and huddle together under my blanket to listen.

Since it was my radio, I got to choose between our only two English music stations. And for a few hours each night, we experienced a whole new world.

The Family produced their own music but their songs weren't about love or loss or pain. Family songs praised Jesus, or our prophet, or the Family itself. The radio brought music and words that made us feel hope and loss. I could live another life in the radio's music, another life where I wasn't so afraid of everyone. Sometimes we'd hear the Cure or the Smiths. I loved the angst-ridden, painful voices I didn't understand but felt pouring into me. Faithy wasn't as enthralled. She liked Cyndi Lauper and Michael Jackson. We'd tap our toes against the footboard until we remembered that we weren't alone, and stopped for fear of waking up the kid on the bottom bunk.

Our secret created a bond and we started talking during the day. We talked about places we'd been and told stories from before, when the cult had been just hippies, traveling in caravans and living in campgrounds, and we remembered being happy. There wasn't much else to talk about. She saw and did everything I saw and did. She was good at remembering movies and as she'd lived in some of the more liberal homes, she'd seen more than I had. She'd tell me the movies, scene by scene and sometimes line by line, like they were stories.

I hadn't made many friends, or at least didn't keep them. I was in trouble a lot and few of the children around me were stupid or brave enough to be friends with someone on the shepherds' radar. Friends in the Family were a liability, but now I had a friend, or something close to it, and I liked having someone to talk to.

Then a few weeks into our nightly listening party, Auntie Mercy caught Faithy in my bed. We'd accidentally fallen asleep. Auntie Mercy didn't see the radio, but she told us she'd better not catch us again. When she didn't say anything to us the next day, we thought she'd let the infraction slide. If she had, it would have been the first and last time she'd shown anyone mercy. I didn't know her well enough yet to fear her as I should have.

'What else?' asked Uncle Stephan. His eyes were cold and blue and he had this German accent, which was perfect, really. I had tried to avoid him, but avoiding him was impossible. I hadn't seen any Nazi movies or I might have known that he fit the mold, like a caricature. His eyes terrified me.

Despite only wearing a thin undershirt, I wasn't cold. Still, I folded my arms over my chest and shivered.

'I was foolish. I told some jokes I know,' I said.

'What else?'

After the first hour, I ran out of things to confess. I was tired and confused. I stopped talking. I didn't know what they wanted. I closed my eyes and I was quiet when I heard his boots on the tile floor. Uncle Stephan always wore boots in the house. No one else ever did. Grandpa didn't like wearing shoes indoors because shoes dragged filth inside and evil spirits could hitchhike on shoes and clothing. 'Grandpa' was David Berg, the founder of the Family. The adults called him 'Dad', which was as confusing as it sounds. In another reality, another time, he'd have been locked up in an institution. In my reality and time, he founded a cult.

I felt Uncle Stephan's breath on my face for a moment. Then he slapped me hard across the face. I heard the shepherds praying for me again, or maybe they were praying against me. I felt my lip with my tongue and tasted blood. I didn't know where my parents were or if they knew what was happening. I didn't dare ask.

I opened my eyes and met his across from me. I hated him.

Uncle Stephan had already put me on silence restriction for a month. I'd only recently been allowed to talk again. We hadn't seen a movie all year because we weren't 'following the spirit'. It's not like we ever watched anything but musicals anyway, but those were better than the nothing we had now. He liked public punishments. And he used a bamboo cane he carried around with him. Spanking wasn't anything unusual, but his cane, which broke skin, only happened behind closed doors. Most of the time they just used a belt or a paddle.

So I stared at his eyes and I didn't blink and I wanted him to see I wasn't crying. I knew he'd break me. They hadn't broken me yet but it was inevitable. All I wanted in that moment was for Uncle Stephan to know breaking me wouldn't be easy. I looked above Uncle Stephan's head and saw a poster of Jesus. This wasn't the blond, friendly Jesus. This Jesus was coming down from heaven on a horse, surrounded by the flames of a burning earth.

If the shepherds had watched any cop shows before they dropped out to follow Jesus, they would have known the proper way to do an interrogation. While I sat in the dining room and tried to figure out what the shepherds wanted from me, Faithy was in the shepherds' office upstairs and probably wondering the same thing. They didn't know they were supposed to tell me Faithy was upstairs and I should tell them everything before she cut a deal. But then again, there were no deals in the Family. Confession, while possibly good for the soul, was not good for my immediate future.

I couldn't think of any more small crimes. So I just started making shit up.

'I took some apricots from the pantry.'

'Why?'

'I was hungry and there were lots so I thought it was okay.'

'What else?'

'I murmured about having to watch the kids instead of going postering last Saturday.' That was a lie, but a lie that might work in my favor. I liked taking care of the little kids. Plus, my mom was in charge of them so being assigned to help with the little kids meant spending the day with her while most of the home was out raising money by selling posters or knocking on doors and asking for donations.

'What else?'

Six hours later, the sun was up and I could hear the home stirring upstairs. The kids assigned to make breakfast walked around the circle of shepherds and me. The kids looked straight ahead as they passed. There was a time when I might have felt humiliated. But we were used to public punishments now so I didn't mind them seeing me. We'd all been in this chair at some point. Those who hadn't knew it was only a matter of time.

The shepherds either had what they wanted from me or gave up trying. Auntie Mercy wanted to pray again. This time I had to hold their hands and the words she prayed told me this was just the beginning of my ordeal.

A few weeks later, still in the attic where they'd decided to store problem kids like me, where we'd read the insane ramblings of our drunken prophet, where they expected us to report every thought that passed through our heads, where the beatings happened daily, I broke. It sounds more like a sigh than the shattering you feel in your soul. I remembered how it didn't hurt when I broke, how it was easier after.

The Romans came that night. But they were too late. Someone tipped off a reporter at the local newspaper, who tipped off the home shepherds. Before the sun rose, we quietly crammed ourselves into vans, kept our heads below the windows, and our shepherds drove us to the next home.

Faithy didn't come to the new home and I knew better than to ask where she'd gone. And now, this woman named Ruthie, with Faithy's face and voice, was asking me about the radio. 'Did they ever find it?'

'You didn't rat me out,' I say. No, they never found the radio.

'But then why did you get in so much more trouble than I did?' she asks.

'I wondered about that for years. But you know how it goes, you just stop thinking about it. Then one day, I was telling my girlfriend about the radio and I finally figured it out. They thought I was gay.'

'Goddammit,' she says, smacking the table. The pearl-snap-shirted Austinites stop to stare at the interruption of their peace. We both smile at the three Family sins she's just committed – drawing attention, unwomanly loudness, and the greatest and least forgivable, taking the Lord's name in vain. 'How much did that suck?'

I laugh and shake my head and say, 'Fuckers.'

This is the shorthand we speak because she knows, without me having to tell her, how hard it was to give them that one thing. To know they were right, even if only once. But at thirteen, I wasn't yet a lesbian, or anyway I didn't know it. Back then I was just an awkward tomboy.

She shows me pictures of her husband, her kids. I show her pictures of my dog. We talk all afternoon. She says she's doing all right. Maybe we're both grading on a curve, but I tell her I am too.

And we don't have to explain. We remember. ∎

Feng Sun Chen

Fly

You have never listened to me, actually.
You are more real.
It would be nice to hang out. I actually don't see people these days.
Maybe once a month, I see a friend.
Every day, I see a monstrosity in the kissing hole.
I don't mind. Everything perfects for a reason.
I want to tell my daughters to forgive themselves.
Through extreme humility, I forgive myself
and through it I forgive my mother.
The woolly bear hurls and perceives worldly shadow,
gains simple understandings
of what was once grey and calcified,
forgets the things that compelled me
as I gain a twisted liberation.

Ken Follett with his parents, Martin and Veenie, and his sister, Hannah, 1957
Courtesy of the author

BAD FAITH

Ken Follett

I was not allowed to go to the movies as a child. There was a cinema in Cowbridge Road, Cardiff, not far from my home, and just about every boy I knew spent Saturday mornings there, watching low-budget serials about cowboys and space rockets, Robin Hood and Lassie. I feel a flash of recognition, now, when I read of Proust's young narrator gazing with longing at theatre posters on the Morris columns of Paris.

I went instead to the public library, a hundred yards away from the cinema in the same street. I probably learned more there than my friends did at the movies, but I did not appreciate that at the time. On the contrary, I was outraged by the prohibition.

We called ourselves the Fellowship, or sometimes the Church of God, but the world knew us as the Plymouth Brethren. This movement split from the Church of England in the nineteenth century. Such groups are as fissile as Trotskyites, and they splintered again and again. I was born into the Needed Truth Brethren, named after our magazine, *Needed Truth*.

Truth is an important word in Protestant sects. Their key text is John Bunyan's allegory *The Pilgrim's Progress*, one of whose heroes is Mr Valiant-For-Truth. Their duty is not merely to seek the truth, but to proclaim it bravely, even – or especially – in defiance of misguided orthodoxy. 'Protestantism' is a literal term: it was always a protest movement.

My father and his brother had married two girls who were cousins, conjoining three already large families, and almost every member of the resulting clan was in the Fellowship, including my four grandparents. It was forbidden to marry outside.

Every sect needs jargon. We did not have churches, we had halls; services were called meetings; the congregation was the assembly; the elders were overseers.

We went to meetings three times every Sunday, and sometimes on Saturday afternoons too. The adults also went on at least one weeknight. I could bear all that, but from a young age I had trouble with the sect's strict Puritanism.

In our house there was no TV, radio or gramophone. These things were 'worldly' – an important term for us. I was often told: 'Our citizenship is not of this world', a saying which paraphrases the letter of Paul to the Philippians, in which he says: 'Our citizenship is in heaven.' This was interpreted to mean that we should not join political parties, trade unions, the armed forces or any kind of social club. The Fellowship paid much more attention to the petty rules of Paul than to the open-hearted wisdom of Jesus.

Another bad word was 'pleasure'. We did not go to the theatre, concerts or sporting events. I recall being told that it was all right to go to the motor show to buy a Gospel Van, but to spend a day there just because I liked cars would be wrong, for it would be nothing but pleasure.

It was an egregious sin to enter a church of another denomination – especially another branch of the Brethren. I learned, many years later, that my father's adolescent rebellion had taken this form. At the age of fifteen, Dad went to a meeting of the Open Brethren. Now, the distance between their beliefs and ours was the breadth of a hair. A brother from another town could take part in our meetings only if he brought with him a letter of commendation from the overseers of his assembly. The Open Brethren, by contrast, would welcome anyone who said he belonged without checking, hence their name. I know of no other difference. And yet my father got into serious trouble.

He was seen coming out of that den of heresy, and it was reported to my grandfather. Grandad Follett, a cobbler with a little shop in Glamorgan Street, blamed too much education, and announced that young Martin was leaving school the next day and would go out and get himself a job. My father, a star pupil at Canton High School, saw his white-collar future fading away. My grandmother viewed this prospect with equal dismay, and pleaded for mercy – successfully. My father promised never to stray again. He had been bullied into keeping the faith.

When he lay dying, he told me he was having sleepless nights, 'worrying about what the future holds'. This shocked me. He knew he had terminal cancer, and I had assumed he felt confident about what would happen to him after death. Is that not the great consolation of religious belief? It seemed he was not as convinced as he had always pretended to be. I did not take him up on this, feeling it would be unkind; but, reflecting on it as I have done often since he died, I wonder if perhaps he wanted me to challenge him. Why else would he have said it? Did he feel the need to confess doubts he had never previously acknowledged? If so, I was too slow-witted to see it. When we mourn, the lost opportunity to say important things is a large part of our sadness.

In my father's adolescence there was another crisis, according to family legend, when a music teacher told Grandad Follett that Martin had the potential to be a concert pianist. From that day my father never had another lesson, for fear that he would have been tempted to go on the stage. That would have been worldly.

For the first ten years of my life I lived in Leckwith Avenue, a cul-de-sac of tiny row houses tucked into the fork of a railway line. The main track to Swansea was at the bottom of our garden, and on the other side of the narrow street was a branch line to Ninian Park, the home of Cardiff City Football Club (to which I was not allowed to go). The embankments front and back formed our playground, and we thought nothing of venturing onto the tracks: it seems a miracle, now, that there was never an accident.

At the closed end of the street was a Scout hall: I was the only boy in the street who was not a Cub.

At the other end was an Open Brethren hall. I peeped in once. It was a plain room with chairs around a central table. On the walls were framed texts, but no pictures, and certainly no idolatrous statues. It looked exactly the same as our hall – but my parents never thought of entering the place. Every Sunday, in our best clothes, carrying our Bibles, we went past the door – three times – and walked another half-mile or so to our own hall in King's Road.

This kind of thing was not uncommon in Wales. There is a joke about a Welshman shipwrecked on a desert island who built two chapels: when he was rescued they asked him what the second chapel was for, and he said: 'That's the one I *don't* go to.'

My uncle Ken left our sect and joined the navy. After this rebellion he repented, and entered yet another splinter group called the Exclusive Brethren. He started wearing a hat, because the Bible (Paul again) says that men should take off their hats in church, and how can you take off your hat if you're not wearing one?

That was just silly, but it was hurtful when he would not sit down at the table with his mother. I recall a fish-and-chip supper at Nan Evans's home in Aberdare when Uncle Ken took his food into an empty room, because to eat with people outside the Exclusive Brethren – even his own family – would have violated the rules.

When my mother died, many years later, Uncle Ken was not allowed to attend the funeral, even though she was his sister, because it was a service of a rival sect. However, several people reported seeing him in the village that morning. He had driven seventy miles just to stand in the street and watch the hearse go by.

Everything we did had to be bent towards the kingdom of heaven, our true home. There was a problem with music, though. Strictly speaking, we should have had nothing but hymns, but we are Welsh, and even the most devout among us found it hard to live on a restricted musical diet. There was always a piano in the house, and both my parents played classical pieces as well as sacred music. Eventually they weakened enough to buy a radiogram. However, rock 'n roll was banned.

It did not take us kids long to sniff out the hypocrisy in that.

American fundamentalists were equally fanatical but smarter, and they produced records that sounded like pop music but had religious lyrics. I recall a swinging number that went something like this:

> This world is not my home
> I'm just a-passin' through
> If heaven's not my home
> Then, Lord! What will I do?

I caused a crisis by buying an album of this kind of stuff, called *Canaan's Land*. The grown-ups hated it but had trouble defending their position. My formidable uncle Eddie said it was jungle music. In response to that I said: 'Uncle Eddie should not criticise other people's forms of worship.' This piece of precocious impudence was repeated all around the family, causing shock but some laughter as well. I did not have the guts to say it directly to Uncle Eddie, but he soon heard of it, and I expected to be carpeted. To his credit, he did not reprimand me, but just looked thoughtful.

I do not have the soul of a Puritan, and I began to disobey as soon as I was old enough to get away with it. I loved movies and dancing on Saturday night and smoking cigarettes. (Tobacco was prohibited as a lust of the flesh.) I bought a guitar, and did not use it to play hymns.

The doctrine was harder to throw off. In my early teens I still believed in the literal truth of the Bible. Everyone in our family read the Bible every day. I followed a course of home study that required me to read all sixty-six books without skipping anything: I had to answer questions on each book before going on to the next.

This did me no harm. Much of the King James translation is by

William Tyndale, one of the greatest-ever writers of English prose. I should have read it twice.

My parents also read *The Times* and *Reader's Digest*. And my father made the crucial mistake of ordering, by mail, *The Reader's Digest Great World Atlas*. I read everything printed that came into the house (I think all writers do this when young), and when I sat down to read the introduction to the atlas I learned about continental drift, the theory that the continents are pieces of a jigsaw that are slowly moving apart over millions of years. And so I began to doubt the Bible, thanks to the *Reader's Digest*.

I felt tremendous guilt about these doubts. I was going against my parents' most profound convictions. The open arguments were all with my father, but the moral pressure came from my mother who, in later life, used to warn my Catholic Filipina housekeeper that she was going to hell.

I was much helped by Edmund Gosse's autobiographical book *Father and Son*, the story of a young man who rejects the Plymouth Brethren. It was a great comfort to me, as an adolescent, to realise that I was not the first boy to suffer these agonies of conscience.

My crisis came over the doctrine that our citizenship was not of this world. Another version of this edict came from Paul's second letter to the Corinthians: 'Be not unequally yoked with unbelievers.' A yoke is a wooden frame placed on the necks of a pair of draught animals so that they can pull the plough together, and Paul's instruction refers back to the Old Testament Book of Deuteronomy: 'Thou shalt not plow with an ox and ass together.' The Brethren were too special to share a task with the rest of the unenlightened world.

A group of adolescents from our assembly, led by one of the overseers, started to visit an old folks' home once a week for an hour on Wednesday evenings. We played board games with the residents and listened to them talk about the old days. They broadened our minds, and perhaps we brightened their lives a little. Incredibly, this activity was judged by the other overseers to be an unequal yoke, and forbidden. By now I was sixteen and able to recognise arrant nonsense when I saw it, and I left the Fellowship, never to return.

I was still a Christian, though a troubled one. About this time I had to decide what to study at university, and I chose philosophy in the hope that it would help me resolve my doubts about the existence of God.

It certainly did. At University College London the merciless light of linguistic philosophy was shone on the ideas of Plato, Descartes, Marx and Wittgenstein. We did not discuss religion much, but privately I applied the tests of evidence and logic to religious ideas. None of them passed. By the time I graduated I was an atheist.

And an angry one. I felt I had been duped. I resented the hours I had wasted at meetings, the childhood without movies or television, the prohibition on joining the Boy Scouts. Most of all I was angry that I had believed the rubbish I had been fed. Nothing is more infuriating than the revelation that one has been stupid.

I also believed they had tried to steal something from me. Making moral decisions is an essential part of what it is to be human. Most people would agree with that, but it carries an implication, noted by the existentialists: if you hand moral responsibility to another authority – the Bible, or a priest or the Pope – you may simplify your life, but you lose a part of your humanity. This is what Sartre calls *mauvaise foi*, translated as 'bad faith' or 'self-deception'.

Philosophy turned out to be the beginning, not the end, of my journey. I'm reminded of Picasso's famous remark: 'It took me four years to paint like Raphael, but a lifetime to paint like a child.' I took three years to become an atheist, and I have spent the rest of my life finding my way back, by an implausibly roundabout route, to a kind of spirituality.

It happened like this. When I started to try to write novels I found I had no vocabulary for describing buildings. To remedy the defect I read *A Concise History of Western Architecture* by Robert Furneaux Jordan. It was the beginning of a lifelong enthusiasm – and more than that.

The most fascinating of all buildings, for me, were the great European cathedrals of the Middle Ages. I began to visit cathedrals and read about them. And I was soon struck by the questions that occur to most people when looking at such a building: Why is this here? Why did the people of the Middle Ages want one of these?

And they wanted them badly. A cathedral cost a fortune – a moon shot is a comparable modern project – yet the men and women who put it up lived in wooden houses without chimneys and slept on the floor. Construction was extraordinarily difficult with hammer and chisel and an iron measuring rod. Just look at the complex three-dimensional curves of a vaulted ceiling, then remember that the master mason had no knowledge of the cubic equations that describe such shapes. And building took decades, often employing multiple generations of masons and carpenters. What drove those people?

I soon began to think that this question might power a long popular novel. There was only one novel, as far as I could see, about cathedral building: *The Spire* by William Golding, which focuses on a monk's spiritual relation to the tower he is putting up. You would be hard put to find two novelists as different as Golding and me, and I felt confident that what I wrote would be nothing like his book.

The Pillars of the Earth is the story of the building of a fictional medieval cathedral, and of the way the construction project changes the lives of everyone in the neighbourhood. Right at the start I saw that the story would have to feature at least one admirable character who is a sincere Christian, if only for realism. I gritted my teeth and created Prior Philip, a very practical monk who cares for the spiritual and material welfare of his people here on earth, and never tells them to suffer patiently because they will be happy in heaven. He is probably the best character I have ever written.

It is a long book, 375,000 words, and it took me three years and three months to write. I found it extraordinarily difficult, and when it was finished I experienced imagination fatigue for the first time.

But the result was on a level different from anything I had written previously, and it found a huge audience. And of course I saw the irony of an atheist writing a much-loved novel about a church.

When I met Barbara, my second wife, I became actively involved in the Labour Party, and I was surprised to find that some of our allies were devout Christians. It turns out that there are many Prior Philips in the real world, anguished by the material and spiritual poverty of some of their neighbours, just as Labour Party activists are. I began to feel embarrassed by my contemptuous youthful dismissal of believers.

My discomfort was eased when the Catholic press attacked Barbara and me for being pro-choice. We were used to unfair reporting from the Conservative papers, of course; in fact, when we were pilloried on the front page of the *Mail on Sunday*, we took it as a sure sign that we were doing something right. But somehow I expected Christian journalists to be more honest. Silly me.

I continued to visit cathedrals long after *Pillars* was finished, and eventually I had to admit that something else was drawing me to these places. Then Barbara became the Member of Parliament for Stevenage. Going to church services is one of the duties of an MP's spouse, but I found myself enjoying them, and began to go when I didn't have to.

I now describe myself as a lapsed atheist. I still don't believe in God, and I never take Communion. But I like going to church. My favourite service is choral evensong.

So today, half a century after I escaped from the Fellowship, I'm a churchgoer again, not regular but not infrequent either. Our thirtieth wedding anniversary happened to fall on Remembrance Sunday last year, and Barbara and I celebrated by going to the service at St Albans Cathedral.

Why do I go? The architecture, the music, the words of the King James Bible, and the sense of sharing something with my neighbours all work together. What they create, for me, is a feeling of spiritual peace. Going to church soothes my soul. And, I have at last figured out, that is exactly what it's supposed to do. What a long time it takes us, so often, to understand the simplest truths. ■

BLUE SKY DAYS

Tomas van Houtryve

Introduction by Eliza Griswold

When Asma Safi, a 24-year-old Afghan woman, died of heart failure in Kabul in 2011, her last wish was to be buried in her grandfather's village in Chapa Dara, a district in eastern Afghanistan controlled by the Taliban.

Asma Safi was my friend and translator, and Chapa Dara was a dangerous place. Its steep cornfields and forests provided the Taliban fighters near total control on the bumpy dirt track that served as the only road into the mountains. The fighters blocked food, fuel and medicine from traveling along that road in order to menace its citizens.

To bury her in Chapa Dara, her father, Ihsanullah Safi, would have to brave the road and return to his home village of Morchal, where he was no longer welcome. He worked for Save the Children, an international NGO that the Taliban opposed. For Safi, taking his daughter home meant risking death at the hands of those fighting against his efforts to build a new and democratic Afghanistan.

Safi went anyway. Loading Asma's body, wrapped in a white shroud, into a taxi, he set out for the mountains. For Safi, there was only one thing more frightening than being seized by the Taliban. The funeral, like any wedding or other event, might be spotted by an American piloting a drone seven thousand miles away at a military base in Syracuse, New York.

'If the drone saw us by the grave, it might kill us,' he told me later, twisting a white handkerchief in his lap as he spoke.

Taxiing past a hangar in the Jalalabad airport, I've seen the snubbed noses of America's Predators in eastern Afghanistan. I've heard them at night while lying on a bed made of floor cushions. The growl of a Predator flying low is something between a lawn mower and an angry jet. Its menace is audible. The sound alone has driven people insane.

For those caught beneath its thrum, there's no comfort that the drone, and whoever is at its helm in America, is only targeting the bad guys. President Obama's drone strikes in Afghanistan have a history of targeting, by mistake, weddings and funerals. The Obama administration claims 116 civilians have died in these strikes; the Bureau of Investigative Journalism puts this figure higher, at 800.

In 2012, one such civilian, Momina Bibi, was outside her house in north Waziristan picking okra, locally called 'ladies' fingers', when the sky filled with the noise of death. There's no way to know whether Bibi, which means sister, looked up at the last minute, and if the American operator caught sight of her face and realized his mistake before killing her. Wounded by shrapnel and prompted by outrage, her thirteen-year-old grandson, Zubair Rehman, traveled to Capitol Hill in 2014. At a small meeting with lawmakers, he said, 'I no longer love blue skies. In fact, I now prefer gray skies. The drones do not fly when the skies are gray.'

In an act of quiet rebellion, the photographer Tomas van Houtryve went onto Amazon.com and bought his own drone, a quadcopter, with which he began to photograph, above the United States, the kind of events that the pilots of Predators and their commanders accidentally target: weddings, groups of people exercising, people praying or attending funerals.

The result is his unsettling collection of photographs, *Blue Sky Days*, which frame the occasions that Afghans, Somalis, Yemenis and others have come to fear. Devoid of easy sentiment and without captions, these lonely images capture an essential vulnerability, laden with the menace a Predator implies.

Ihsanullah Safi decided to risk the funeral for his daughter, Asma. He refused to deny her the honor of a proper burial even if it meant that he too might lose his life. Standing by the grave, he grew even more concerned as local Taliban, wearing the black turbans he feared were easily seen from above, began to gather as a gesture of respect.

After the funeral, Safi visited the local Taliban commander, who'd lost his own son in a drone strike not long before. He tried to talk to the commander about his strong daughter, Asma, and a new Afghanistan in which, under one flag, Afghans as different as they were could build a new country together. The commander didn't listen. Enraged by his son's death, he was all the more committed to America's. ■

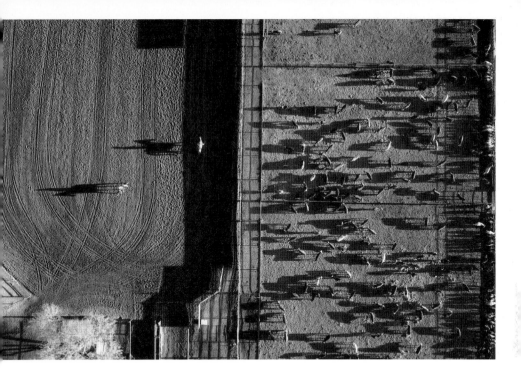

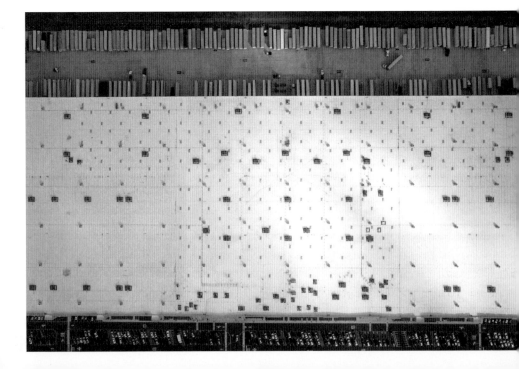

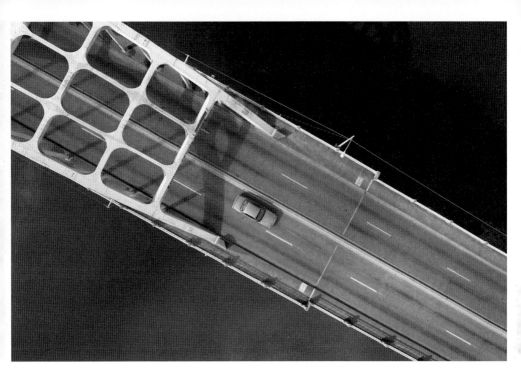

GRANTA

THE MAGAZINE OF NEW WRITING

PRINT SUBSCRIPTION REPLY FORM FOR UK, EUROPE
AND REST OF THE WORLD (includes digital and app access).
For digital-only subscriptions, please visit granta.com/subscriptions.

GUARANTEE: If I am ever dissatisfied with my *Granta* subscription, I will simply notify you, and you will send me a complete refund or credit my credit card, as applicable, for all un-mailed issues.

YOUR DETAILS

TITLE ....
NAME ....
ADDRESS ....
POSTCODE ....
EMAIL ....

☐ Please tick this box if you do not wish to receive special offers from *Granta*
☐ Please tick this box if you do not wish to receive offers from organisations selected by *Granta*

YOUR PAYMENT DETAILS

1) ☐ Pay £32 (saving £20) by direct debit.

   To pay by direct debit please complete the mandate and return to the address shown below.

2) Pay by cheque or credit/debit card. Please complete below:

   1 year subscription: ☐ UK: £36   ☐ Europe: £42   ☐ Rest of World: £46

   3 year subscription: ☐ UK: £99   ☐ Europe: £108   ☐ Rest of World: £126

   I wish to pay by ☐ CHEQUE ☐ CREDIT/DEBIT CARD

   Cheque enclosed for £_____ made payable to *Granta*.

   Please charge £ _____ to my: ☐ Visa ☐ MasterCard ☐ Amex ☐ Switch/Maestro

   Card No. ☐☐☐☐☐☐☐☐☐☐☐☐☐☐☐☐

   Valid from *(if applicable)* ☐☐ / ☐☐   Expiry Date ☐☐ / ☐☐   Issue No. ☐☐

   Security No. ☐☐☐

SIGNATURE .... DATE ....

Instructions to your Bank or Building Society to pay by direct debit

BANK NAME ....
BANK ADDRESS ....
POSTCODE ....
ACCOUNT IN THE NAMES(S) OF: ....
SIGNED .... DATE ....

DIRECT Debit

Instructions to your Bank or Building Society: Please pay Granta Publications direct debits from the account detailed on this instruction subject to the safeguards assured by the direct debit guarantee. I understand that this instruction may remain with Granta and, if so, details will be passed electronically to my bank/building society. Banks and building societies may not accept direct debit instructions from some types of account.

Bank/building society account number

☐☐☐☐☐☐☐☐

Sort Code

☐☐☐☐☐☐

Originator's Identification

☐9☐☐1☐☐3☐☐1☐☐3☐☐3☐

Please mail this order form with payment instructions to:

Granta Publications
12 Addison Avenue
London, W11 4QR
Or call +44(0)208 955 7011 Or visit
GRANTA.COM/SUBSCRIPTIONS for details

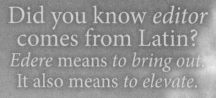

THE INTERPRETERS

AMONG THE BRAHMINS OF BENARES

Aatish Taseer

'The past has to be seen to be dead; or the past will kill.'
– V.S. Naipaul

1

When I first came to Varanasi seventeen years ago I came by overnight train. It was only a distance of some eight hundred kilometres from Delhi, but it was not merely physical; distances in India rarely are. And the long journey made more real the other aspect of the distance, its cultural and historical dimension, the feeling of travelling across centuries. It was a big humid summer night, brightly lit and filled with mosquitoes. The train had a romantic name, the Kashi Vishwanath Express. Its carriages were striped in two shades of solid blue, the names of passengers printed and glued to the outside. The platform was crowded with travellers, now asleep on their luggage, now sharing food from polythene bags. We travelled through a darkened landscape dotted with red-brick buildings bathed in fluorescent light. In the morning, a sun of dull gold rose through tinted windows. The air in the sleeper grew close. There was the intimacy of waking up among strangers, some stirring, some belching frankly. All this had been a preparation of sorts, the slow acknowledgement of distances that were not merely physical.

Things are different now. Physical distances have evaporated even as cultural ones have deepened. The IndiGo flight takes no more than fifty minutes. The airline, with its jaunty punning – the in-flight magazine is called *Hello 6E* – and its air hostesses in dark blue, with matching slim leather belts and pillbox hats, is part of the spread of a modernity whose depth is hard to gauge and whose trappings suggest attitudes that aren't necessarily there. The hostess serving me a Junglee chicken sandwich – Sweetie is her name – has a pin on her sleeve that says GIRL POWER. But that does not mean that she believes in, or even knows about, feminism. And let's say she does: it is no guarantee of a unified world view. The same person who has come around to girl power need not believe in gay power, which might well appal her. And even if this sealed-off world of Western freedoms has come down to her whole, there's nothing to say that she is not steeped in Indian caste prejudices. Rationality itself might have only a limited hold on her. She may alternate easily between Western values and a second consciousness made up of faith, magic and astrology.

The reverse could just as easily be true. It may well be that ideas from the West have made quiet inroads into Sweetie's world view and that they now stand in conflict with the values of her parents, or even her own values, which she cannot justify, but which nonetheless have a jealous hold on her. The point is: there's no telling. Surfaces cannot be trusted; they are not an accurate reflection of the country's interior life. In this time of flux, old India roils away under the surface – Nehru's palimpsest country in which, 'one under the other, are written many facts, ideas, and dreams, without any of them completely covering that which is below'. And Sweetie, as if wanting to let me in on the secret, wears a second badge on the same sleeve, which diminishes the effect of the first, and speaks less to female empowerment than to some vague actressy notion of glamour. It says LEADING LADY.

We fly through a thin light-suffused mist. The land below is parcelled out into smallholdings. A golden oval of sunlight sweeps searchingly over the cabin walls. We land among mustard fields, whose little yellow flowers are attractive against the pink and white of the airport's boundary wall.

The studied cool of IndiGo airlines has enforced a civility on the passengers, suppressed certain instincts, which, now that the plane is on the ground and we are close to disembarking, return with force. There is a small stampede at the front and loud talking on the telephone. The South Koreans on our flight who have come to Varanasi as part of a Buddhist pilgrimage – the Shakyamuni Buddha gave his first sermon a few miles away – retreat in the face of these rough manners. It reminds me of an ugly episode a few hours before, on the ground in Delhi. A Frenchman, in grey trousers and a red sleeveless sweater, had pushed past me in the line for the security check.

'Are you going to cut ahead?' I said. 'Would you do this in France?'

He gave me a Gallic shrug, a *tant pis* of such contempt as only the French are capable of.

I said, 'You're very bad-mannered.'

'Don't teach me,' he replied. 'Indian manners!' and vanished ahead, into the crowd.

Manners are the least of India's problems. They will come. But there is a deeper reckoning that must be had.

2

The hermetically sealed world of the airport falls away suddenly. With no warning we are in deepest rural India. The car speeds out into sugar-cane and mustard fields. There are clay houses with red-tiled roofs and low red-brick walls that enclose empty plots of overgrown land. The walls are covered in advertisements for mobile phones and soft drinks, for bootleg educational courses and aphrodisiacs. A line of single-storey shops, their dark fronts hung with bright pendulous packets of pan masala and potato crisps, appear along the edge of a thinly tarred road.

The city thickens around us. There are open drains, channelling gurgling streams of cloudy water, and paper kites wheeling against a grey polluted sky. The shops sell cheap clothes and kitchen things. A wheelbarrow with a pyramid of red gas cylinders blocks our way. The infrastructure crumbles; political posters and religious flags hang limp on this windless December day.

We cross a black-watered drain, garbage on the surface eddying out in a paisley shape. Degraded as it is, this is a sacred boundary: the Varana River which, along with the Asi (now poisoned too), encloses all that is Varanasi – Benares, as it is still known locally; Kashi, as it has been known for millennia.

Near the Taj Hotel the congestion eases. We enter an area of heavy trees and boulevards, bungalows and churches. This is the Cantonment – an aloof and scolding memory of the British presence, which began here at the end of the eighteenth century. There is a statue of Vivekananda, painted a garish copper colour. In 1893, when he represented Hinduism in Chicago's World's Parliament of Religions, he roused the West to the power of India's greatest export: spirituality.

The sight of the statue returns me to 24 April 2014 – the day Prime Minister Narendra Modi arrived to file his nomination papers. Modi is not from here, but he chose the city as his constituency because in the Hindu imagination it is possessed of the power of Rome or Jerusalem: not a mere political capital, but a cosmic one. It is the epicentre of Hindu pilgrimage, a point where all the holy places of Hindu India are symbolically represented. 'Kashi is a place that gathers together the whole of India,' wrote the historian Diana L. Eck in *Banaras: City of Light*. 'Kashi is a cosmopolis – a city that is a world.' The city is a metaphor for old India, in its entirety, and that is why it now serves Modi's politics of revival.

On that day two years ago, Modi moved slowly through Varanasi, stopping to pay his respects at a number of statues along the way. It was a blistering morning of soaring white skies. Bits of white paper and swirling clouds of dust rose and fell over the sweltering streets. The shopfronts were shuttered; the city seemed almost to be empty. I rode pillion on the motorbike of a friend and it was only at intersections that I could see the crowd snaking its way to where Modi was. Later, when people asked me how many had come, I found it hard to say. The city did not have vistas enough for me to gauge the numbers, but it was as if all of Varanasi had showed up to see Modi.

Now the statue of Sardar Patel – India's first home minister and recently a Hindu Nationalist alternative to Nehru (less colonised, more muscular) – is once more just a statue; no longer part of a constellation of figures that Modi garlanded on his way to filing his nomination papers. A wreath of marigolds hangs from his neck. The flowers are shrivelled, the petals a deep burnt red, a memory both of heat and the passage of time.

'Are the good days here?' I say to my driver, half teasingly. ('Good days are coming' had been Modi's slogan.)

'It will take time,' he replies, his mouth swollen with the thick granular remains of a betel chew in its late stages.

The old city – a warren of narrow streets through which arteries have been forced – now begins to close around us. Soon there will be that first view of the water. During these months away, months in New York, I spent hours looking out of my window imagining that first glimpse of the riverfront. I had to actively stop myself from grafting the geography of one city onto another, imagining the Ganga in place of the Hudson, which takes a momentary turn north in Varanasi, flowing back towards its source in the Himalayas; ghats instead of piers; cremations and bathers on the West Side Highway; the tight conglomeration of the Manhattan grid replaced by the labyrinth of sunless streets. And what could be easier than to imagine, in place of New Jersey, a sandy waste delimited by a pale line of trees?

That first sight of the city curled around the river goes through me like the breath of something old and known and familiar. The city has been destroyed many times in the last thousand years, no less by development authorities than by conquerors. And yet it is so perfect an articulation of the culture that built it that the overlay of centuries has not muffled its voice. It still stands, still speaks. It enshrines a spirit that could only have belonged to old India: a temple town set along the banks of a broad river staring frankly into the void.

3

I wake before dawn to the loud pealing of a bell outside. A solid one-note toll at 4 a.m., without let-up. I don't mind. It is the hour of Brahma, a time famously conducive to those engaged in intellectual work; and since that is in part what I am here for, I think, why not! I lie in bed listening to the bell. Despite the hour and the cold of the December morning, there is footfall outside my window: people are making their way down to the Ganga.

The breath of the river, which can always be felt pressing against this house, is heaviest now. A sluggish cross-weave of ripples goes over the water. The brightening of day corresponds to a quickening of activity on the riverfront. The first flecks of pink in the dark oily water bring the first bathers. The air is soon high with the sound of bells and conches. A film song, crackling and morose, carries from a radio. A broken column of orange appears on the water. The day does not so much brighten as it exposes. And there is always a little dismay, akin to what we might feel on walking into a room in a house where a party was held the night before, at the first sight of squalor. It is so pervasive, so all-encompassing, that it seems as sourceless and inevitable as the broadening of day itself. A black bitch, with flapping udders, licks clean the yellow remains of potato curry from a heap of used leaf-plates. There are white and pink plastic bags, like dead jellyfish, on the edge of the water.

The river, as with Varanasi itself, is endowed with mythical power – it runs between this world and the next. It is holy, but not out of reach; it is threaded into the daily life of the city. And there is something marvellous about seeing a grown man lose himself in the sanctity of the river. Arms spreadeagled, he splashes it repeatedly, as if preparing it for his ablutions. Then he dunks himself and pirouettes with his hands raised. He digs at the water with folded hands, pushes it away from him, as if shadow-boxing with an imaginary enemy. It is difficult for me to enter into the symbolic and ritual power that the river holds for him. He scuttles off to the bank and returns with a small clay lamp burning in his hands. He turns and turns in a clockwise motion, the smoky flame trailing after him. When his compact with the river is complete, he leaves the lamp burning in the dark earth, a testament to the vows he's made. It is a small perishable memorial, Joycean in its beauty and banality, to how one ordinary man began an ordinary day.

I am staying at the Alice Boner House. She was a Swiss artist and scholar who lived in Varanasi for decades. She came from a wealthy Swiss family – her uncle was one of the founders of the engineering firm Brown, Boveri and Co. – and she was soon disenchanted with 'the pert, lewd atmosphere' of Paris in the 1920s. In 1926 she saw Uday Shankar dance in Zurich: 'Evening in the Kursaal: a lot of kitsch, and a revelation, the Indian dancer,' she wrote in her diary. In Shankar, she saw 'a living source of Indian sculpture'. They became lovers and she came with him to India for the first time in 1930. Six years later she returned to live in this house on the Ganga, which is now an institution for visiting writers and painters. She lived here until a few years before her death in 1981. Her work, her library and her diary provide entry points into the deeper life of this city – where it is still possible to see an intact medieval life, full of pilgrims and students of classical grammar and language, seekers of all kinds.

It is a source of shame to me that, despite having lived most of my life in India, the world of tradition in a city like Varanasi is closed to me. And the reason is plain: I am colonised. I am part of that class which the British administrator Lord Macaulay set out to create in the 1830s: men who would act as intermediaries 'between us and the millions whom we govern'. Indian in blood, English (and now increasingly American) in tastes and intellect. Macaulay was roughly my age – thirty-four – when he was appointed president of the Committee of Public Instruction, and he knew that he could never educate the whole body of the people. His plan was to create a class that would gradually extend modern knowledge to the great mass of the population. But that is not what happened. What happened instead was that this class grew more isolated with every generation, more deracinated – Gandhi described them as 'foreigners in their own land' at the opening of the Banaras Hindu University in 1916.

At the time of independence, when an old culture was being reborn as a modern nation, there was a moment when this imbalance might have been corrected. It might have been possible to profoundly reform the system of education the British bequeathed us, which had been borne out of an open contempt for Indian learning and antiquity, and which had the ultimate aim of creating 'a nation of clerks' to serve the British Empire.

But the opportunity was not taken. India's elite was culturally and linguistically denuded. We had ceased, in India and Pakistan, to be bilingual. Out of a private effort, I had regained Urdu well enough to translate, and I was a student of Sanskrit; but the knowledge of these languages would forever be incomplete, and this deepened my sense of what had been lost. I grew up as one among many who lived in India but dreamed of the West.

It is difficult to fully capture the strangeness of the experience; one can really only gesture at it. I have a picture, for instance, of myself, aged eighteen, on my first trip to Varanasi. My hair is cut short and I am sitting on the stone steps of the riverfront, dressed in a flimsy black long-sleeve shirt covered in white Oms: ॐ (I found the mystic syllable on my keyboard!). I'm wearing baggy pants and sandals. What is clear from the picture is that I have understood my mother's desire for me to go to Varanasi as encouragement to adopt a kind of fancy dress. I am a Western traveller, a modern-day hippy in search of secret India.

It is a perfect example of what a curator friend in New York describes as the South Asian need to 'self-orientalise'. The analogue would be a Frenchman who has lived in France all his life, but hardly knows any French. He does not know Molière or Racine or Balzac; he has never visited Chartres or Reims. Then, aged eighteen, his mother decides, just as he is going off, *comme il faut*, to college abroad, that it is a disgrace how little he knows of his culture, and demands he make a pilgrimage of sorts, an internal grand tour.

But – since he has no model for how and why these places should be visited – he goes down to the nearest tourist shop, buys himself a PARIS, JE T'AIME T-shirt, puts on a Georgia Tech baseball cap, a pair of New Balance sneakers, straps a money belt round his waist and sets off to see the sights at Strasbourg, say, or the chateaux of the Loire Valley.

The British colonisation of India is nothing, either in scale or vehemence, with the colonisation independent India made of itself after the British left. It has pursued the aims of the colonisers with a dedication that would have surprised Macaulay. The result is a ruling class that is hard-wired to reject India. It would be the equivalent of an elite in Europe and America that was systematically steered away from all aspects of European culture, language, art and literature: bred in the bone to turn their nose up in distaste at the mere mention of Homer or Dante or Shakespeare.

The power of this class was not its own; it was an extension of the power of the West. It made India feel like an outpost, and it created an atmosphere of cultural apartheid.

In Delhi I witnessed this scene:

A fashionable woman – lunching at a new restaurant in a mall – finds her pasta is not al dente. She calls over the waiter. He is happy to replace it, though he doesn't really know what is wrong with it, just as he would not have known what was right with it. He reaches in to take her plate, but she stops him. It is not enough that he replace her pasta. Does he understand, she wants to know, the meaning of this phrase, al dente? He reaches in again for her plate. No, she says, her cruelty now sublimated into gentleness, she wants him to learn. Does he even know the meaning of this phrase, al dente? No, he confesses, he does not know what it means and, quaking now, reaches in again for her plate. She won't let him take it. Not till she's done talking him down. For a moment the waiter believes the scolding is really about the food. Now he sees, as it grows in tenor and scope, what is really happening. 'Asiatic resignation' – Evelyn Waugh's phrase from *Vile Bodies* – enters his face. He can smell the woman's wish to diminish him. Otherwise why ask: What village is he from? What does his training consist of? Is he really qualified to be serving this food? She has seized on this little phrase, al dente – no doubt come down to her from a holiday abroad – in order to crush him: to expose him for the servant she knows him to be.

Underlying the woman's contempt for the man is contempt for the country he comes from – which, incidentally, is her country. Her contempt, in this case urban and class-based – India has infinite systems of inequality: exquisite composites of class, caste, language, education and wealth – prevents her from seeing that, far away from the mall, is a country that knows all that it needs to know about food – about its preparation, its serving, its quality. But in India the knowledge of foreign things does not begin with a knowledge of one's own things; old India is not the foundation, nor ever the inspiration, for modernity: to be modern is to renounce India. The transition strips uncolonised India of its confidence, as it has this waiter. It creates a new class of interpreters, to which the woman belongs, who will impose a new tyranny of borrowed things, a new club to which ordinary Indians can only hope to be part of if they forsake much of what is dear to them, from language and dress to culture and worship. The relationship between old and new is broken: to be modern is to come empty-handed into an unfamiliar world.

4

Those on top feel infinitely secure; but this security is an illusion. The Modi election itself had the quality of a revolution at the ballot box; the power of the English-speaking classes, as represented by the Congress Party and the Nehru–Gandhi dynasty, was undermined. And, in Pakistan, where society has a similar shape, I had seen first-hand, in the murder of my father, how this class war, if denied an outlet in democracy, could take a more violent form.

My father was a Pakistani politician who had spent a long time out of politics. When, in 2008, after a gap of some fifteen years, he was made Governor of Punjab, the country's largest province, he returned to politics in a place that was radically changed. The decade after 9/11 had given Islam an ugly new vitality. The religion had become a kind of armour against a modernity that felt alien, impure and threatening. It served as a front in the class war against men like my father.

A chance set of circumstances, behind which there was a certain inevitability, brought matters to a boil. A few months into his new job, my father took up the cause of a Christian woman who had been condemned to death for blasphemy. He spoke out against the severity of Pakistan's blasphemy laws – he called them 'black laws'. He thought he was protected by his class and stature – he joked in drawing rooms about how the clerics had declared him *wajib al-qatl*, the Islamic designation for a man fit to die, a man any good Muslim may kill. His position was in fact more precarious than he realised. The judgement of clerics and television hosts came down on him. He became a blasphemer himself in the eyes of many. Then, one dismal January afternoon in 2011, as he was leaving a restaurant, his bodyguard shot him dead.

The story was nothing if not a lesson in the fragility of the power of the colonial classes. The bodyguard became an instant hero in Pakistan. Lawyers showered him with rose petals hours after he'd killed my father; ordinary people sent him food and money in jail; they named a mosque after him; they had their children blessed by him. It was impossible for my father's killer to be brought to justice. And when, after great difficulty, he was tried and executed in February 2016, a crowd the size of a small North American city poured into the streets to bid him farewell. A media blackout could not prevent it from becoming one of the largest funerals in the country's history.

During the killer's trial, his lawyers, trying to justify what he had done, gestured to my father's 'lifestyle . . . character and associated matters'. It was a coded way of saying that he was liberal, educated and Westernised. He was also part of Macaulay's class of interpreters. A version of that class existed all over the old non-European world; and, regardless of whether that social and moral order was desirable or not, the power of that class was untenable. It was bound to be broken. It is not possible to live at such a remove from one's country and still hope to survive.

5

In Varanasi I am looking for someone to take me out of myself, out of my isolation, my hesitations and reserve. One evening, as the traffic of bathers and loafers gets going on the riverside, I meet Shivam Tripathi.

He stands out from the group of four or five Brahmins he is with. He is dressed in a saffron lungi with a matching scarf, and a grubby jacket. His forehead is marked with two fierce points of red. His *shikha* – the tuft of hair that is the mark of the Brahmin – is thick and oiled, tightly knotted. I notice him first because of the drama of his appearance, and then because I can feel the force of his gaze on me. He has a fine-boned face downed in a light growth of brown hair; his teeth are stained from tobacco; there is a kind of feral intensity about him.

Shivam comes from a family of poor peasant Brahmins in Madhya Pradesh, a Hindi heartland state of uncommon beauty. He arrived in Varanasi as an eight-year-old to learn Sanskrit. 'I've lived all over the city,' he says, with the trace of a smile. His intensity lies coiled in him, ready to spring. From the moment he hears why I'm in Varanasi – I say I'm interested in the conflict between tradition and modernity – he stops me in my tracks. 'The conflict,' he says, 'is not between tradition and modernity. It is between modernity and spirituality.' The word he uses – *adhyatmikta* – is important; it is derived from atman, which is cognate with the Greek *atmos*, and means 'self'. It implies an idea of spirituality that is less prescriptive than that of the Abrahamic religions. It is closer to the classical notion of 'Know thyself', which Oscar Wilde tells us 'was written over the portal of the antique world'. In old India, too, it was the great message of the Upanishads: the personal self was a site to discover the supreme self; spirituality and self-discovery were inextricably linked.

No sooner has Shivam set me straight than he wants urgently to show me something. It is as if he can tell that I have been too long in my head and have failed to see – or, rather, *feel* – something important.

And then we're off, at a fast pace, through the tight labyrinth of streets. I'm dimly aware of passing mosques with enclosed gardens, where the azan is now sounding. Through the iron bars of little alcove temples a smoky electrical light wafts out. I have not yet acquired the local ability to walk without stepping into something dreadful. My eyes are fixed on the paving stones, now wet with paan spittle bleeding into puddles – bits of styrofoam floating in the reddish water – now smeared with cow shit. The paving stones are covered in urine stains, large and brown and frilled, like great wilted carnations. The air is high, and then, with that Indian genius for contraries, it is in turn overwhelmed by cloying waves of jasmine.

The scene around us is changing. The temples are suddenly garish; I get a glimpse of Tamil script. Shivam explains that we are entering the south Indian quarter of the city. From the increase in human traffic and the appearance of souvenir shops and flower sellers, it is clear that we are approaching a major temple. The evening tide of worshippers sweeps us along. Shivam's room-mate, a student of classical grammar, has joined us. The temple appears at the end of a long bulb-lit street.

In the interior courtyard the cold marble floor is marked with the black impressions of bare feet. The two Brahmins press their heads against a stone at the entrance of the temple and enter with the ease and familiarity of someone entering their own home. We pass many smoke-blackened subsidiary shrines before coming to a statue of Kali. The two Brahmins, wrapping one leg around the other, while holding the lobes of their ears in a gesture, at once fearful and reverent, squat low before the dread goddess. Shivam takes me into the central sanctum, to the great scarified head of the Kedareshwar linga. It sits in a brass casement and is among this city's most powerful representations of its ruling deity, Shiva. It is not smooth and polished like the others, but dark and rutted, a domed outcropping of rock, with a single white line running through it. The head is ringed with cloudy water and strewn with leaves, marigolds and tiny white flowers. Shivam sinks to his haunches and drinks the water euphorically. I touch my head to the linga. Before I can look up, he smears my forehead with cool streaks of sandalwood paste. It is a gesture of great warmth and spontaneity, a bringing in of someone who is clearly out.

Unsaid between us is an understanding that I am to try to apprehend what is happening here, in the sanctum, by a faculty other than the one I use normally. So when I stop midway to ask Shivam the name of the leaves, he looks at me with annoyance. He tells me they are bilva leaves – *Aegle marmelos* – and gives me the verses from scripture, which say that they are dear to Shiva, but I'm missing the point. Faith functions by an internal logic; it is its own means of knowing and one does not know by asking questions; one knows by feeling.

As if wanting me to recognise this, Shivam now throws his head back, closes his eyes and begins to sing. He sings beautifully, in praise of the goddess Durga, bringing the song to an end with: 'Shiva, Lord of All, who resides in Kashi, O Ganga.' This last word – Gange, in the vocative – is drawn out. Shivam ends his praise of Shiva with a Sanskrit verse, the metre sounding out like a shot in the sanctum, sombre and stilling.

Then he leads me out from the back of the temple into the open night air. The steps going down to the river are bathed in white floodlight. A pilgrim boat is arriving, full of middle-aged women, who hitch up their saris and begin to trudge up the steep stairs. Shivam turns to me and says with disdain, 'Look, that is our modernity.' I hadn't noticed, but behind us some teenage girls in jeans and pink socks with busy designs on their sweaters are taking selfies, screaming and giggling as teenage girls everywhere do. 'And that,' he says, now pointing down the steps, towards the river, 'is our *adhyatmikta*.' On the edge of the river, where there are a few floating lamps, I can just about make out the figure of a man meditating. He sits with his back to us, draped in wet saffron, still as a rock.

'Either we throw ourselves into this modernity,' Shivam says, almost hatefully, 'or we go back to what we were; what is intolerable is this limbo, this middle condition. In the end' – he points down the dark arc of the river – 'the truth is only that.'

Through the thick murk of a December evening, the roaring orange fires of the cremation ghats are visible.

6

In every other Indian city, the cremation ground is profane, polluted and placed outside the city. But not here. Varanasi is the supreme cremation ground and here the cult of death, as Octavio Paz writes, 'is also a cult of life, in the same way that love is a hunger for life and a longing for death.'

The ubiquity of death in Varanasi at first made me resistant to it; it seemed like a thing for tourists. And there they were, on the Harishchandra Ghat, photographing the disarray: the corpses in their bamboo biers, wrapped in gold cloth; the wood piles; the dark exposed earth; goats, roaming about like teenagers from the 1980s, in baggy T-shirts of sackcloth. It is a grotesque commingling of light and shade: there are puppies and little boys slapping the grey ribbed belly of a reposing cow next to mourners in white, with little peaked Nehru caps. Through the screen of smoke and dirty orange fire, women in the near distance wash clothes on a smooth slab of red stone, twisting the cloth into what look like thick coloured strands of twine. The soap mixes with the ash; a mother or sister removes nits from the hair of a child; there are wheeling birds on the river and stony-faced ascetics who watch the scene from their haunches, like old park-benchers waiting for the next game of chess.

To die in Varanasi is to break free from the cycle of rebirth. That is the promise of Shiva, whose city this is. The Kashi Labh Mukti Bhawan is a place where people come to die. It is a lovely red-brick building, picked out in yellow, with a porch and green louvred windows.

We sit in the winter sun outside this house of death, or of freedom, depending on how you look at it. The old Brahmin manager is dressed in nothing but a yellow woollen vest and a lungi. He is reading the newspaper – the *Dainik Jagran* – over which lies a red-lettered religious text. He has cropped grey hair, stubble and smooth thin arms which he rubs from time to time as he speaks. 'There were once many such houses in Benares.' Then, as if anticipating his detractors, those who feel it is now an unpardonable act of blind faith for poor people to come all the way to Varanasi to die in the hope of attaining nirvana, he adds, 'It is a difficult road, and when it gets too hard, people say it's a fraud.'

Inside a woman is dying. Her small nacreous eyes peer out from the top of a thick brown blanket. Despite their murk, they show signs of recognition and curiosity, courage and fear. Her son, a sixty-five-year-old science teacher from Bihar, is reading to her from an epic poem, detailing the deeds of Ram; but his mother's hearing is gone. The reading, like the small sips of water from the Ganga that are poured into the old woman's open mouth, is a ritual act. It had been the old woman's long-standing wish to die in Varanasi, and her son had made true on that wish. He had brought his mother here to be free. Her illnesses are behind her, the son says; she has stopped eating; only death awaits. And part of what makes this scene so moving is that this man who loves his mother is now forced to welcome her death.

'Think how hard it must be,' someone whispers in my ear, 'to wish the death of one's own mother.'

I am about to leave when the son begins to cry. 'Give me your blessings,' he says, 'because now I have no mother.'

Outside, in the central courtyard, the sun comes in through the top, casting a pattern of dots and long bars across a whitewashed balustrade, blackened and peeling in places. From a pretty semicircular transom some coloured glass pieces have fallen out. *Hare Rama, Hare Lakshman* plays through the house.

The Brahmin manager at the house of death knew the culture encircling him would bring into being a world where every day there would be fewer who might frequent the house. He knew, too, that this encirclement was not culturally neutral; it was a transmission from the West, and a great part of its appeal rested on the power of science, medicine and technology. The body, he said, was a *vastra,* a vestment (the words are cognate); he now reused the image in a more interesting way. He said, 'I can understand the need for doctors and engineers. And where there is necessity, I can understand why one would have to wear a shirt and trousers. But why not leave it there? Why not,' he adds, 'come home and change back into one's Indian clothes? Why imitate their fashions? *Why not,*' he said, with the desperation of a man determined to have it both ways, to take the fruits of modernity and guard oneself from its values, 'be Indian at home and Western outside?'

7

The Indian failure is of an old culture, decaying for centuries, that will neither die nor serve as inspiration for the future. That miraculous moment, when the seed of something very old fertilises the present moment and produces something utterly new, has not happened. The past is dead weight, and Indian modernity skin-deep, like a top soil that bars access to the nutrients of the deeper earth, but which cannot itself sustain life.

Shivam, who had come all the way from a small village in central India to study the Vedas at Banaras Hindu University, understood this failure. He asked himself what would become of those who studied Sanskrit there. What would become of Sanskrit itself, in this country?

It was a deceptively simple question. What he was really asking was: would India move into the future with no thought to her past? Would old India simply be forsaken? And if so, what would the future look like?

We were sitting in his tiny room, which he shared with two other students. The floors were strewn with rugs and mattresses. On a low table to the side, bound cheaply in red, were the great books of classical India: grammars, treatises, epics, the Vedas. With its atmosphere of medieval scholarship, it was like a scene out of Chaucer, unspeakably moving. I remember thinking that this was what an education in the humanities might look like if only some distance could be created, and if a man like Shivam could come to this learning from a spirit of intellectual enquiry and not piety.

In the corner was a picture of Kali, red-tongued and fierce, with a small Shiva linga in front of it. The Brahmin students did all their own cooking, and there were little plastic jars of spices, a small gas stove, a rolling pin, some dry flour. In the courtyard outside a great tree had died, the same tree that gave us the bilva leaves that were so dear to Shiva. Its branches cast long shadows over the powder-blue walls of the house. The courtyard was overrun with weeds and half hidden in the undergrowth were the carcasses of an old generator and an air cooler, its broad blades rusting in the open air.

8

I had started out with an intimation of how precarious my situation was in India, a sense of my rootlessness and isolation. But I had the West to turn to; Shivam had nothing. And his situation was far more precarious than mine. He had a young wife, and a child – he hadn't told me! – who were staying with his in-laws. He was worried about his ability to provide for them and had considered taking up some basic priestly work in a small temple. His grand education had not prepared him for modern India. He had no English, no skills; he wanted desperately to be in politics, and was trying to build a constituency by helping people in his area – a low-caste man in a neighbouring village who needed money from the government to build a house, a young Brahmin boy who wanted an education akin to the one Shivam had received. Shivam knew only too well how undesirable a path this was.

Shivam and I represent two poles in a world increasingly divided between globalised elites with shared values and cultures, and heartlands which are culturally and economically dispossessed. This dispossession produces rage, which can express itself as a hateful and irrational urge to have the West pay for the way the East looks. There is the very real physical degradation, the small flyblown towns with foul air, the poisoned water bodies, the dusty flyovers, the open drains, the treeless dug-up streets, desolate but for giant advertising boards. This is what modernity actually feels like in these parts, and it is not so much an advertisement as the signs of an impending calamity. This vision of urban apocalypse corresponds to a deeper intellectual and spiritual crisis of a culture unable, even after centuries, to digest modernity. The failure is one of translation: old India has not found a way to pass on the germ of its genius. And as long as old cultures fail to find a path to renewal, no one – least of all Europe – will be spared the rage of people who knew they were once something, and whose confidence has been broken.

Shivam wanted me to see the old country in its death throes; the young people crushed by the conflict between modernity and *adhyatmikta*, the spirit of old India.

'Let them see someone like you,' he said, 'who is modern through and through. Then they will understand this terrible middle state they're in. If you want to see living Indian culture, you have to come to my village.'

9

It was many weeks before I could take him up on his offer. The December murk was gone. The days were sunny, the sky cloudless, the city reappeared from the haze, a vision liquid and enduring, a mixed promise of change and continuity.

We left Varanasi at dawn on Makar Sankranti, the day in the Hindu calendar when the sun begins its northern course, a day of festival. Shivam's friend, Rohit, a student of classical grammar, came with us, on his way to Maihar Devi, a place of pilgrimage not far from Satna. The two Brahmins were dressed in jeans and sneakers. Shivam wore a little maroon-and-beige-checked jacket, with some meaningless words on the back – STYLE RIGHT, THESTEREOS COPIC FEETING. It was almost a kind of disguise. Save for their *shikhas*, and the occasional glimpse of a sacred thread, they were indistinguishable from any number of idle young men who roamed the riverside at night. Nothing in their appearance spoke of the many fine ideas and considerable learning – much of it ready on their lips – that had been instilled in them from childhood. In this sense, though I loathe the phrase, they really were part of a secret India, part of the interior life of a country that has been pushed inwards, and which now finds no means of expression.

As the Sri Lankan art historian A.K. Coomaraswamy had felt a century ago: India misunderstood Western modernity. It treated the 'concrete and material achievement' of Western civilisation as an end in itself, and 'endeavoured rather to imitate results than to assimilate methods'.

It had produced a world in which India sat in wait of what the West had to give it. The idea of contribution hardly existed. India did not innovate, not even in the sciences and technology; India merely offered up her millions to do the grunt work of the developed world. In return India received a ready-made modernity, which she grafted onto the Indian scene. The meeting of this kind of pre-packaged modernity and India was not combustible, nothing like the meetings of cultures India had known in the past. It was inert, a clean denial of India's distinctiveness and originality. When one entered its spaces, described by the economist Amartya Sen as 'islands of California in a sea of sub-Saharan Africa', one found people who in speech, dress and manners were crushingly unsure of themselves. The contrast between this laminated world and the real India was staggering: outside, people's language was still vivid; inside, they spoke an English that was almost an impediment to communication, a lifeless jargon, in which word and meaning had parted ways. Outside, they dressed with an effortless elegance, using colour with a painter's confidence; inside, they had been reduced to drab formulas. One might argue that a moment would come when the energy of the outside would fertilise the inside and India would devise a modernity every bit her own, but it was impossible to believe this based on what existed on the ground now. Indian modernity, to which globalisation had added steroidal power, felt like a shroud, an ill-fitting garment that muffled the Indian voice.

Rohit left us in Satna, a dreary cement town, treeless and bleak, with a municipality that was at once overactive, now digging up the roads, now laying new cables, *and* – where it mattered – totally absent. Satna was an unplanned, low-lying sprawl of self-wounding ugliness, with streets choked with traffic and filth. And though it presented about as catastrophic a vision of urban life as it was possible to conceive of, it could not be ignored: for the simple reason that more and more every Indian town looked like this.

It was evening when we reached the village of Domhai. A cement road, lined with a fencing of bramble, curled out among fields of young wheat, mustard and chickpea. The car nosed its way past clay houses with low red-tiled roofs. Shivam's house was pink-washed, with high pointed alcoves. There was a small sacred plant at the entrance – *tulsi, Ocimum sanctum* – on a whitewashed base fashioned from the earth. Shivam's mother, going about her evening prayers, soon emerged with a single smoky lamp, a plate and a bell. His father, a sturdy Brahmin farmer, with a dyed moustache and white stubble, welcomed us with a garland of hand-picked flowers. The house was dark, with earth floors and smooth undulating walls. A single weak-rayed bulb in the kitchen hung over a television set playing news of a terrorist attack in Indonesia.

That evening we wandered the dark streets of Domhai. The families we visited, many of whom were related to Shivam, all had televisions. They alternated between the news in Hindi and religious sermons. These two elements – politics and faith – formed a circle, one feeding the passions of the other. It was what had propelled Modi forward. The village had basic electricity twenty-two out of twenty-four hours a day. Everyone had mobile phones. But its days were numbered. The village, which had sustained so much from the connection to the land, to the life of tradition and ritual and the social organisation of caste, could no longer sustain itself.

That night, in the village shop, which sold biscuits and light bulbs and practically nothing else, there was a palpable sense of despair. The young men in tracksuits who had gathered around, some sitting on sacks of grain, some on wooden benches, could speak of nothing but the uncertainty of rural life. Modernity had reached them in the form of technology – which, if anything, exacerbated the need to get out of the village – but it had also reached them in the form of a changing climate. One handsome farmer, bearded and bawdy, said in thick dialect, 'The seasons are no longer on our side.' Then, laughing, he added, 'The man up there, he either gives with all his heart, or he takes with a stick up your ass.'

The next day we found ourselves bumping along on a bad road, on the way to the temples at Khajuraho. It was dark outside. The clay houses, with their naked bulbs, appeared fairy-lit. The darkness made Shivam maudlin and confessional. I was struck by how clearly he could see that India's problems were cultural. At the same time he seemed not to recognise the inevitability of the transition his world was going through. 'Perhaps we do need modernity,' he said, as if it were optional, 'but it must use our existing culture as its foundation. We cannot erect a second sun in the sky only to find that we ourselves have been destroyed.'

We reached Khajuraho by daylight. The temples had once been weather-beaten and wild, but the Archaeological Survey of India had – to use Neel Mukherjee's phrase – given the temple complex a 'municipal soul'. There were flower beds full of dahlias, and little cemented pathways. Some temples had even been rebuilt. I recall thinking that in places where the religious past lives on, where it is still wrapped up in the perfume of worship, there is no joy in contemplating one's distance from it. That joy – which is intellectual – comes only to those for whom the past is no longer fused with faith, and for whom it is not sacrilegious to consider its ravages with a dispassionate eye.

Shivam was at home among the temples and there was something marvellous in watching him thread his way through the complex. He greeted the deities with loud salutations as he entered their sanctum; he touched everything; he sang, he dozed; in one temple, he reached past the iron grille to anoint his forehead with some ash from an incense stick. It gave me a pang. I had done a great deal on the level of language and reading to close my distance from my country. But, even after a lifetime, it would never allow me to know India as those for whom the past was still alive knew it. Neither of us was in an enviable position: not Shivam, with the vestiges of his grand culture, for which modern India had made no place at all; and not me, who had spent the majority of my adult life undoing the effects of a colonial education that isolated me from my country. Shivam had his culture, but it would not get him anywhere in modern India. I had been stripped of mine; and though my background was an advantage in the globalised world we inhabited, I could not let go of my sense of loss. We were both looking for a way out of the nightmare of history, both trying to salvage a sense of self without making a fortress of that self.

Britain, modernity, now globalisation – if one wanted to go further back, then Islam too – they had all washed over India, and India had endured. Sometimes it felt as if that was all India had done: India had endured. Her endurance was something of a miracle, and it never ceased to inspire wonder. 'Greece, and Rome, and Egypt – all extinguished,' wrote the poet Iqbal. 'And yet we remain. Not easily erased, though the tides of time have forever been our enemy.'

I, for my part, found it amazing to consider the British presence in India, now that its legacy among the people – the small 'class of interpreters' I belonged to – had been superseded, and Britain itself was going headlong into a new and deeper state of irrelevance. The 'class of interpreters' managed to exert their power so long as prosperity was limited. But now that wealth was spreading to deeper levels of society, one came face-to-face with the realisation that Britain might in fact have left quite a thin imprint in India. The country, in her languages, her culture and religion, had remained largely herself. And the more time passed, the more it seems that this great historical event – British rule in India, whose legacy has wasted the energies of generation after generation of intellectuals and academics – could simply be shrugged off. It might come to seem like little more than a regrettable accident, a misadventure shrouded in mutual embarrassment.

India's own historical problem, however – the problem of what to do with the past – would remain. There is more to civilisation than endurance; there is vitality and strength. And that is why so many friends of India, and admirers of her past, have wished nothing more than for the end of old India to come quickly.

10

In my last days in Varanasi, I was haunted by the memory of a man I had met eighteen months before.

The Samaveda school is in the north of the city. The streets here are of a different quality – quieter, cleaner, the buildings in better shape. It is possible to follow the unbroken line of a cornice along a pale blue facade, or to admire the ironwork of a slim balcony jutting into the street. I came in from the glare of a hot April morning to a shaded courtyard with green-painted columns. The young Brahmin boy who showed me in was dressed in two measures of white unstitched cloth. He led me past great rusting metal cupboards, through corridors hung with the pictures of former gurus.

He explained that Gyaneshwar Shastri, his guru, had a high fever. But he would speak to me nonetheless, because he was a teacher and it was his dharma to teach. Dharma, like atman, is another of the great untranslatable Indian words. It can mean duty, religion, vocation; but it is also the dharma of fire to be hot and of water to cool. Shastri's dharma was to teach the Samaveda – the Veda of song, and the one dearest to Shiva – and he knew nothing else.

I found him reclined near a shrine in the far corner of the courtyard, where the air was smoky. He wore a loincloth and a sacred thread. His body was wrinkled and sinewy, and his white beard had yellowed in places.

I was interested in the life of tradition, but it was an irony about this journey I was on that many of those in whom tradition was most intact were least able to speak of it. They could not see themselves from the outside. What mattered was the example of their life, and this particular life had been so cloistered, so walled in by tradition, that it made conversation hard. We lacked a shared vocabulary.

Shastri was bound in by a changing world, quite literally circummured. What did he have to say to the society beyond the walls of the Vedic school? What did tradition have to say to modernity?

But Shastri was not even aware of what lay outside the walls of the school. Tradition, like faith, works by an enclosed, private logic. It is self-contained, and it nourished him completely. In fact the only indication he gave me of the world beyond was when he told me that we were living through the last of the four great Hindu ages – Kali Yuga – an age of decline and unrest, followed by dissolution.

I thought I would ask him, since our conversation was running into dead ends, what the value was of teaching the Vedas in this age of darkness and ignorance.

The question roused his interest. This was language that meant something to him. He now knew exactly what I was talking about. He looked at me through the glaze of his feverish eyes, then he said, 'Do you know what beej raksha is?'

It literally means 'the protection of the seed', but Shastri seemed to be speaking of it conceptually; and no, as a concept, I did not know what it meant.

'During the rains,' Shastri said, 'when the land is flooded, the farmer will take the seed' – he made a pouch with his hands – '*and* he will put it in some high place, where it is safe from the waters. Then, when the flood retreats, there will be farming again.'

He held my gaze a moment longer, and said, 'This is what we do, and this is all that can be done.' ∎

The blurred snapshot presumed to be Ivan Chistyakov, from the NKVD files.
Courtesy of ELKOST International Literary Agency

DIARY OF A GULAG PRISON GUARD

Ivan Chistyakov

TRANSLATED FROM THE RUSSIAN BY ARCH TAIT

9 October 1935

A new stage in my life:
10 p.m. It's dark and damp in Svobodny. Mud and more mud. The luggage store is cramped and smoke-filled. A prop holds up the sagging ceiling, people sprawl on the floor. There is a jumble of torn quilted jackets with mismatched patches. It's difficult to find two people who look different, as they all have the same strange expression stamped on their faces, the same suspicious, furtive look. Unshaven faces, shaven heads. Knapsacks and trunks. Dejection, boredom. Siberia!

The town hardly lives up to its name.[1] Fences and more fences, or empty land. Here a house, there a house, but with all the windows shuttered from the outside. Unwelcoming, spooky, depressing, cheerless. My first encounter: not a smart, upright soldier of the Red Army but some sort of scruffy partisan in a shabby greatcoat, no tabs

---

[1] The town of Svobodny (which means 'Free') was the headquarters of BAMLag, the Baikal–Amur Corrective Labour Camp administration, part of the GULag system.

on his collar, scuffed boots, cap plonked on his head, rifle over his shoulder. The local community hotel is a village house partitioned into cramped rooms. Overheated. Incessant snoring.

10 October 1935

Morning. I walk down Soviet Street. Unmetalled, no pavement. More fences, pigs, puddles, dung, geese. I could be in Gogol's *Mirgorod*, but this is Baikal–Amur Mainline Railway Central.

HQ is a two-storey brick building, with flower beds and a modern electric clock. Road signs: two reflective triangles and a 30km speed limit. Same mud. Hostel. More mud.

First night in my life feeding bedbugs. Cold. No discipline here either. Incessant swearing.

'Panteleyev, don't give me that crap. Malingering, that's what it is. You know what we call that?'

We call it a crime.

Swearing to the rooftops, incessant, so dense you could lodge an axe in it.

VOKhR, the Armed Guards Unit. Bunks, coloured blankets, illiterate slogans. Some men in summer-weight tunics, some in winter tunics, jackets quilted and not, leather or canvas or string belts. They lie on their beds, smoking. Two are grappling, rolling around locked together, one with his legs in the air, laughing, squealing. Another laments his lot with a wheezing accordion, bawling, 'We are not afraid of work, we just ain't gonna do it.' Men cleaning rifles, shaving, playing draughts, one even managing to read.

'Who's on duty here?' I ask. 'Me,' another partisan replies, getting up from poking embers in the stove. He's wearing padded winter trousers, a summer tunic, winter felt boots, and a convict's hat back to front on his head with a tuft of ginger hair sticking out. There's a canvas cartridge pouch on his belt.[2] He starts trying to tidy himself up, shifting from foot to foot, uncertain how to behave. I find out later this sentinel has never been in the army and only had a few months' training on the job. What a hero! Few of them are any better.

What am I doing here? I ask myself. I feel ashamed of the little square lieutenant's insignia on my collar tab, and of being a commander, and living in 1935 across the road from the nationally celebrated Second Track of the Trans-Siberian Railway, shamed by a brilliant, soaring concrete bridge.

22 October 1935

I spent the night in a barracks hut. Cold. Killed a louse. Met the platoon commander. He seems pretty thick, etc. Walked back along the railway track.

My thoughts are all over the place, like pages torn out of a book, shuffled, stacked, crumpled, curling like paper on a fire. I'm disorientated. Lonely. Sad.

Twenty days ago I was in Moscow, alive, living my life, but now? There's no life here. There's no telling how high the clouds are, and it's impossible to take in the endlessness of the hills and the emptiness of the landscape. One hill, then another, then another, then another, on and on for thousands of kilometres. It's bewildering. Life starts to feel insignificant and futile. It gives me the creeps.

Moscow! Moscow! So far away, so out of reach!

---

[2] The uniform for staff in the GPU (later NKVD) prison camp system, as specified by GPU Order 207 of 21 May 1923, was: greatcoat with red collar tabs and red piping; jacket and jodhpurs, dark blue with red piping; cap with dark blue band and red piping. Not everyone in the security services was an established NKVD staff member; some were prisoners, so they could be dressed variously. It is also possible there was simply a shortage of regulation items in the store at the time.

Freezing temperatures. I hope they finish the earthworks on the bridge soon and I'm moved somewhere else. A comforting thought, providing I ignore the possibility it might be somewhere even worse.

23 October 1935

I slept all night in the warm. The joy of sleeping without needing a pile of bedclothes.

The day greets me with a stiff breeze as I walk along the track. *Zeks* grafting, inching towards freedom with every cubic metre of earth they shift and every metre of rail they lay, but what do I have to do to get demobbed? I didn't wash today: no water. Tomorrow? Probably still none. I can only dream of steaming in a bathhouse. Bathhouses make you happy. Bathhouses are heaven.

24 October 1935

Autumn is all around. There are haystacks, and the first ice on the Arkhara River appears. Autumn is brown. The haze above the distant hills merges with the horizon and you can't make out the sky, what are hilltops, what are rainclouds. A steady wind blows constantly and the oak leaves rustle in lifeless synchrony. The sun does shine, but it's pale and cold, a nickel-plated disc you can stare at. Was I really born to be a platoon commander at the Baikal–Amur Mainline forced labour camp? How smoothly it happened. They just called me in and sent me off. Party members have the Party Committee, the factory management and the trade union to intercede, so Bazarov gets to stay in Moscow. For the rest of us, nobody puts in a word.

26 October 1935

A raging wind drives the thunderclouds low. Autumn! The russet
incline of the hill is hacked into a cliff face day by day, exposing layers
of geology. Trucks drive up, and moments later drive away, shuttling
without respite between hill and railway station. The people, like ants,
are patiently, persistently destroying the hill, transforming its hump
into a square in front of the future station. The gash widens: fifteen
hundred workers are a mere sprinkling in the maw of the hill, but
their crowbars and shovels are having an impact. They count the
cubic metres, fighting for the right to live outside, to be free. They
rush through everything, whatever the weather. There is a hunger to
work and work and work.

There are only statistics, statistics, statistics.

Days, cubic metres, kilometres.

If their strength did not give out, these people would work here
night and day.

They work a ten-day week.

The USSR is impatient for the Second Track. The Soviet Far East
is impatient for goods.

The Second Track will open up this region, speed its development.
And so on.

29 October 1935

Rain and slush. The clay has been churned into sludge, which makes
walking tough. Today is a footslog day. Twenty kilometres to Phalanx 13.

We've been invited to dinner by the section commander.

We walk into the village and enter a huge Ukrainian-style house
that has been plastered from the inside with clay then whitewashed.
Icons are draped with embroidered linen. The bedstead is a trestle

bed with a lacy coverlet and the pillows are in grey chintz pillowslips. Everything is incongruous: the rags stuffed in windows where the glass is missing, the Russian stove, the icons, the bed. Dinner is different too. We have borscht with meat from a goat slaughtered yesterday, then noodles in milk with white gingerbread, home-made with butter. The Ukrainians are in their third year here and have a smallholding with a cow, three pigs, ten chickens. Sometimes they even have honey. Life could be worse for them.

The guards are permanently in a foul mood because their food is so bad.

'They're stashing food away for Revolution Day, so we get no fats.'

The camp administration have everything: meat, butter, everything.

In the evening we get an escape alert and everyone fans out. I walk along the track towards Ussuriysk. It's very still. The sun hovers over a hilltop, its last rays playing over the russet-brown leaves of the trees, creating fantastic colours that contrast with equally fantastic shadows. It's exotic scenery for a European: a dwarf-oak forest, the hills receding, one higher than the other far into the distance, their summits fanciful, humped animals. The haystacks look like the helmets of giants half rooted in the soil.

Construction of the Second Track is nearing completion. Only yesterday this was a graceless, jagged precipice with gnarled shrubs jutting out of it, but today? Today a women prisoners' brigade appeared and now for 150 metres there is an even, two-storey-high embankment with regular lines and a smooth surface that is a sight for sore eyes.

Hills are sliced through, marshes drained, embankments embanked, bridges straddle streams coaxed into drainage conduits. It's the result of concrete, iron, human labour. Stubborn, persistent, focused labour.

And all around, the taiga, the dense forests of Siberia. As Pushkin never said, how much that word contains! How much that is untouched, unknown, unknowable! How many human tragedies, how many lives the taiga has swallowed up. I shudder when I think about the trek to Siberia, to exile, to prison. And now here is Petropavlovka, a village whose buildings bear the mark of a past of direst penury, but where a collective farm now thrives.

30 October 1935

To the bathhouse, the miraculous bathhouse! It's just a wooden shed, its inside walls pointed with cement, although you could stop up scores of cracks and still be left with as many again. There's a layer of slime on the floor, a cauldron plastered in place on top of the stove. The bathhouse is warm now, but how will it be in winter? The roof leaks – but still, I have a good scrub. It feels so good after twenty days!

I couldn't help getting nostalgic over the bathhouse in Moscow. It would be so nice to have a proper night's sleep too, but we are here to work. Nightfall brings disturbances, escapes, killings. For once, though, may the gentle autumn night extend its protective mantle over the captive. Two runaways this time. There are interrogations, pursuits, memoranda, reports to HQ. The Third Section takes an interest, and in place of rest night brings unrest and nightmares.

1 November 1935

Then there are prisoners who refuse to go out to work. They're just the same as all the others, no less human. They get just as upset at losing that roving red banner as anyone else.[3] They cry just as bitterly. They have the same psychology as anyone serving a sentence, the

---

[3] A mark of distinction awarded temporarily to the winning team in a 'socialist competition' contest.

same oppressive thoughts about back-breaking toil, bad conditions, hopes for the future. The same faith that some day they will be free, the same disappointed hopes, despair and mental trauma. You need to work on their psychology, be subtle, be kind. For them kindness is like a second sun in the sky. The competitiveness here is cut-throat. A foul-up in recording their work credits can drive them to attempt escape, commit murder, and so on. No amount of 'administrative measures' help, and nor does a pistol. A bullet can only end a life, which is no solution, and a dead prisoner can cause a lot of grief.

A wounded *zek* is a wild beast.

4–5 November 1935

Five hours' sleep in the past forty-eight. It snowed during the night, icy cold. At five in the morning there's a noise, a knock. I hear the duty guard reporting to the deputy head of GHQ that it's not easing off. It's as cold in the room as outside in the snow.

We check out the huts. Oh, life! How can you do this to people? There are bare bunks, gaps everywhere in the walls, snow on the sleeping prisoners, no firewood. A mass of shivering people, intelligent, educated people. Dressed in rags filthy from the trackbed ballast. Fate toys with us all.[4] To fate, none of us matter in the slightest.

They can't sleep at night, then they spend the day labouring, often in worn-out shoes or woven sandals, without mitts, eating their cold meals at the quarry. In the evening their barracks are cold again and people rave through the night. How can they not recall their warm homes? How can they not blame everyone and everything,

---

[4] A reference to N. Kozlov's popular song of 1859, 'The Fire of Moscow Roared and Blazed' ('Shumel, gorel pozhar moskovskiy'), in which Napoleon looks down ruefully from the Kremlin walls.

and probably rightly so? The camp administration don't give a damn about the prisoners and as a result they refuse to go out to work. They think we are all bastards and they are right. What they are asking for is the absolute minimum, the very least we are obliged to give them. We have funds that are allocated for it, but our hoping for the best, our haphazardness, our reluctance, or the devil only knows what, means we deprive them of the very minimum they need to work.

10 November 1935

This life is nomadic, cold, transient, disordered. We are getting used to just hoping for the best. That wheezing accordion underscores the general emptiness. The cold click of a rifle bolt. Wind outside the window. Dreams and drifting snow. Accordion wailing, feet beating time.

12 November 1935

An influx of juvenile delinquents: the *zeks* call them 'sparkies'. We count them: five short. Count them again: still five short. We check them again: ten short, so another five have got away. We bring out extra security. Thirty sparkies are working; there is no way any of them can escape. We count again: twenty-nine. They cover themselves with sand or snow and, when everyone else has left, come out and leg it. Three more escaped during the night.

I talk to their top dog.

'Can you find them?'

'Sure!'

He did. They won't do it again. It turns out he sent them off himself and they got drunk but they're back now. Others will do the same tomorrow. I let a man out for a pee and he just disappeared. I saw a woman standing there. She pulled out a skirt she'd tucked into her trousers, put a shawl over her head, and before I knew it she'd vanished.

13 November 1935

I walked to Arkhara this morning. Twenty kilometres hardly counts here. We talked shop: someone got killed, someone else got killed. In 3 Platoon a bear ripped the scalp off a hunter and smashed up his rifle. They bayoneted it.

I bought frozen apples. They were a delight to eat. I spent the day hanging around at the station, which is regarded as normal. What can you do if there are no trains? Hang around.

16 November 1935

It's 26 degrees below zero and a gale-force wind is blowing. Cold. Cold outside, cold indoors. Our building seems to have more holes than wall. The building's superintendent comes in and cheers us up:

'Don't worry, lads, it's going to get twice as cold as this.'

How wasteful human mismanagement is. Nobody thought to lay the subgrade before the frost came and now the labourers are forced to dig a trench, 30cm deep, into frozen clay as viscous as tin.

17 November 1935

Do you know what it feels like to be out in the taiga at night?

Let me tell you. There are oak trees, perhaps three hundred years old, their branches bare, like giants' arms, like tentacles, paws, beaks of prehistoric monsters, and they seem to reach out to seize and crush anyone they can catch.

You sit round a campfire and the flickering shadows make all these limbs look like they're moving, breathing, animated, alive. The quiet rustling of the remaining leaves and the branches tapping other branches make you think even more of the Cyclops or other monsters. You are overhearing a conversation you can't understand. There are questions being asked and answers given.

You hear melodies and rhythms. The flames of the fire pierce the darkness for five metres or so, and sparks fly like long glow-worms in the air, swirling, colliding and overtaking each other. The face of your comrade opposite, vividly lit by the flames against the backdrop of the night, with shadows darting from his nose and the peak of his Red Army helmet, looks theatrically grotesque. You don't want to talk loudly. It would be out of place. You want to sit and doze and listen to the whispering of the trees.

23 November 1935

One more day crossed out of my life in the service of pointless military discipline. What if the Third Section read these lines, or the Political Department? They will interpret them their way.

24 November 1935

Have you seen the sun rise in these hills?

Something unexpected is the way the darkness disappears instantly. You look one way and it is dark, then you turn, close your eyes for a moment, and it is day. It's as if the light had been stalking you, waiting for you to open the door so that it could slip in, as iridescent as mother-of-pearl. The sun has not appeared yet but the sky is already ablaze, not only on the horizon but everywhere. It is aflame, changing like a theatre set under the skilled hand of a lighting technician; as the action unfolds, it is painted every colour. Rockets explode, firing rays of light from behind the hilltop. There is a stillness, a solemn silence, as if a sacrament is to be administered that cannot be celebrated without it. The silence intensifies and the sky reaches the peak of its brilliance, its apogee. The light grows no brighter but, in an instant, from behind the hill, the fireball of the sun emerges, warm, radiant, and greeted by an outburst of song from the dawn chorus.

Morning has broken. The day begins, and with it all the vileness. Here is one instance: there is a fight in the phalanx, a fight between women. They are beating one of the best shock workers to death and we are powerless to intervene. We are not allowed to use firearms inside the phalanx. We do not have the right even to carry a weapon. They are all 35-ers, [5] but you feel sorry for the woman all the same. If we wade in there will be a riot; if they later recognise we were right, they will regret what they have done. You just get these riots. The devil knows but the Third Section doesn't. They'll come down on us and bang us up whether or not the use of firearms was justified. Meanwhile, the *zeks* get away with murder. Well, what the hell. Let the prisoners get on with beating each other up. Why should we get their blood on our hands?

27 November 1935

This is how we live: in a cramped room furnished with a trestle bed and straw mattress, a regulation-issue blanket, a table with only three

---

[5] A reference to the inmates sentenced under Article 35 of the 1926 Penal Code of the RSFSR as 'elements harmful to society'.

out of four legs and a creaky stool with nails you have to hammer back in every day with a brick. A paraffin lamp with a broken glass chimney and lampshade made of newspaper. A shelf made from a plank covered with newspaper. Walls partly bare, partly papered with cement sacks. Sand trickles down from the ceiling and there are chinks in the window frames, door, and gaps in the walls. There's a wood-burning stove, which, while lit, keeps one side of you warm. The side facing towards the stove is like the South Pole, the side facing away from it is like the North Pole. The amount of wood we burn would make a normal room as warm as a bathhouse, but ours is colder than a changing room.

Will they find me incompetent, not up to the job, and kick me out? Why should I be sacrificed like so many others? You become stultified, primitive, you turn into a bully and so on. You don't feel you're developing, either as a commander or a human being. You just get on with it.

4 December 1935

Before I am even out of bed, another escape. I'll have to go looking for him tomorrow. We should just shoot three in each phalanx to put them off the idea. Escapes disrupt everything. What a dog's life, sniffing around like a bloodhound, browbeating everyone all the time. Banged one *zek* up for twenty-four hours.

7 December 1935

I have to admit, I am growing into BAM. Imperceptibly the environment, the way of doing things, the life are sucking me in. Perhaps inevitably.

Tried studying Leninism but it only made me feel worse by rubbing in the kind of life we are living. What positive thing can I occupy myself with? Nothing.

8 December 1935

Above the hills there are whirlwinds and snowstorms. Everything is milky white. The silhouettes of trees make it look as if they are walking towards us as, now here, now there, the blizzard relents. But then there's another flurry, and tongues of dry, prickly snow inflict thousands, millions of venomous snakebites. Branches as thick as your arm, thicker even, snap off readily in the icy cold.

I sleep soundly and wake up refreshed. The air is clean and frosty and sometimes there is even a dusting of snow. My lecture programme flaps on the wall. By lunchtime the temperature is down to minus 40 and the cold attacks every exposed part of my body. I stare longingly at a log of firewood, imagining the energy, the warmth within it. It's so cold in the room that a wet hand freezes to the door handle. Soap doesn't lather until the heat of my hand has melted it. Smoke from a steam engine doesn't disperse but hangs in the air like tufts of cotton wool. It mixes with steam to form snowflakes, an impenetrable haze obscuring a window like nets.

The lads have formed a jazz band with penny whistles and pipes, balalaikas and rattles. Music can also be warming, literally.

Meanwhile, *zeks* are on the run. Freedom. Freedom, even with hunger and cold, is still precious and irreplaceable. They may get away for only a day, but at least they get out of the camp. I wouldn't mind a day away from this job myself.

9 December 1935

Minus 42 degrees during the night and very, very quiet. The air chimes like crystal. The dry crack of a gunshot. It feels as if the air could break like glass and splinter. In places the ground has fissures as wide as my hand. It's so cold that even the rails can snap, with a sound unlike anything I've ever heard.

29 January 1936

My neck has frozen up and I can't bend or turn it. I have a headache and a runny nose. Went out to Territories 13 and 14. Squad Commander Sivukha goads his grey along at a gallop but my devil of a horse, snorting and twitching its ears and straining at the reins, doesn't let me take the lead.

My heart is so desolate, it alarms me.

I feel as if I'm not living in the real world but in some weird, unearthly world in which I can live and think but can't speak my thoughts. I can move, but everything is constrained. The sword of the Revtribunal hangs over everything I do. I feel constantly held back: you mustn't do this, you mustn't do that. Although I feel solidarity with society, I feel cut off from it by an insurmountable, if fragile, partition. I'm aware of my own strength, yet at the same time feel weak and powerless, a nonentity. I feel hopelessness and apathy, almost despair, that so much cannot be achieved. I stumble blindly along the paths of this world, unable to work out what is allowed and what is not. The thought that drills into my brain is, How long will this go on for? A lifetime? I have at least ten years of life ahead of me and I'm not being allowed to live them like a normal human being. Must I despair? We have to fight for every stupid little thing: a visit to the bathhouse, sugar, matches, clean linen, and more besides. As for heat, firewood, we almost risk our lives for that. We, the armed guards, are powerless.

5 February 1936

The sun warms us more kindly, and is even quite hot. During the day it gets as warm as 15–18 degrees. Not long now until summer and more escape attempts. The shortages of food, shoes and underwear are so tiresome. We are promised everything, and in the Centre they clearly think we are living in a paradise. In reality, we are living in theories. We have theoretical semolina, butter and new uniforms. Theoretically the Centre is thinking about us. That's supposed to be encouraging. For some reason I simply do not believe it. Perhaps I'm the wrong sort of person. I would like to be provided, simply and without rhetoric, with the basic necessities. Today we had dumplings and home-made noodles, etc. Tomorrow, it will be home-made noodles and dumplings, and that has been going on for the past month.

11 February 1936

Making a little joke out of it, just barely hinting, the political adviser mentions mentoring. Incentivisation. If a phalanx fulfils more of the Plan, the platoon commander gets paid more. I'm not swallowing that bait. How could I be a Stakhanovite[6] when I have no wish to work at

---

[6] The Stakhanov movement took its name from Alexey Stakhanov, a worker who allegedly mined fourteen times his quota of coal on 31 August 1935. The Soviet authorities claimed the movement increased labour productivity by 82 per cent during the Second Five-Year Plan of 1933–7.

BAM for more than a year? If you stand out then you will never get away. In any well-ordered project you find some disorder, but we have more disorder than order. They put pressure on the guards and hint at incentivisation, but make no attempt to address the real problem. There are all these miscellaneous 'educators' in the Education and Culture Unit slobbing about, getting drunk and generally behaving scandalously, and the guards are expected to cover for the job they are not doing.

The phalanx leaders have it in for the guards. Our superiors are supposedly rehabilitating *zeks* and we're supposed to just put up with it. Why doesn't someone put those people in their place and stop them undermining our authority! If you dismissed me now without a month's notice I'd agree to it in a flash. In fact, I'd agree to donate a month's pay on top. What sort of work can you do in that kind of mood? All the same, I wonder what they do with educated people who would be capable of managing a phalanx, teaching them and so on.

12 February 1936

Today is a holiday in Moscow. I would be riding the tram home, planning my evening.

13 February 1936

The hills, the taiga, my thoughts, all exist in a kind of vacuum. Not only that, but a vacuum with constraints. There is another world abroad. I know it exists, but I can't get there.

23 February 1936

Red Army Day. I hand over 5 Platoon and prepare 4 for handover. Something is in the air. I'll be somewhere, somehow. I don't like moving, carting my belongings around, settling in. I'll even miss 4 Platoon a bit. They weren't such a bad lot.

25–26 February 1936

In Zavitaya. Spent a sleepless night in a truck. I feel doped all day. The boss calls me in and appoints me commander of a division. I've drawn the short straw, I'll have to serve in this army for decades now, like a serf. I sit with Savchuk and listen to the gramophone. It's emotionally unsettling.

I receive my letter of appointment. I have to start forming a divisional HQ. I have a meeting with the men from Moscow. Someone has a keen ear and long tongue. The company commander alludes to my demob yearnings. It feels strange, after the taiga, to be in an actual town. I'll have to get used to it. I'm not feeling quite right in the head. Must be the sleepless nights.

Also the jubilation, the wild, throbbing jubilation, has thrown me off balance. I receive a greetings telegram to mark Workers' and Peasants' Red Army Day. I'll enter . . . [sentence left incomplete]. The violin reduces me to a quivering wreck. There's nobody to exchange so much as a word with. There's no one to answer my questions.

I can't do this. I can't.

My pen is blunt.

Just breaking off in mid-sentence. ■

Kelly Schirmann

Your Youth

When I was nineteen
I heard *Another World Is Possible!*
This was long before the answer
was a new system of packaging
that more closely resembled leaves
We walked & walked
in the other world's cities then
Across the bright white desert
of Imagined Economic Desert
White Men With Dreadlocks
like wild animals, roaming freely
Like political bumper stickers
& sea water in the open air
It was confusing, the suggestion
of having an enormous power
I heard her echoing from the future
Your Youth Is Meaningless!
& I was delighted to find it was true
I have never been in love
with so many variants of nothing
I ate what I could
I wish just one song
knew how to talk about it

THE TRANSITION

Luke Kennard

In the council chamber, every room looked like a waiting room, lined by low oblong benches and school chairs, one strip light flickering. It was hard to get up from the deep spongy bench when their mentors came through the double doors of 151.

Karl's first thought was that they didn't look any older than he or Genevieve, but then maybe there was only a decade or so in it. He had expected an aura of age and experience: authority figures, the way teachers looked when he was a pupil. Janna was angular and pretty, a white blouse tucked into a black leather pencil skirt. Her mouth was very small, like a china doll's. Stu at least looked weathered. He was wearing black jeans and a black T-shirt with a lightning bolt on it. He had a black-and-purple Mohawk, four inches tall, five spikes.

'God, this place is depressing,' said Stu. 'Sorry they made you come here.'

'Don't get up,' said Janna, once they were up. They exchanged air-kisses.

'You probably weren't expecting us to look like this,' said Stu.

'Oh, what, the Mohawk?' said Karl.

'The Mohawk actually wore a patch at the base of the skull and a patch at the forehead,' said Stu. 'This is closer to an Iro.'

'Do you have any . . .' said Genevieve. 'Indian blood, I mean?'

'Genevieve,' said Stu, 'I am merely an enthusiast.'

Stu busied himself collecting four flimsy cups of coffee from the machine in the corner. The two couples sat opposite one another over a pine-and-clapboard table too low for the seats.

'Drink,' he said. 'It's terrible, but, you know, ritual. Everything feels better when you're holding something warm. You're a primary-school teacher, I'm told?'

'That's right,' said Genevieve.

'That's brilliant,' said Stu. 'You're one of the most important people in the country. And Karl?'

'You know those flyers you see stuck to lamp posts that say MAKE £1,000 A WEEK ONLINE WITHOUT LEAVING YOUR HOUSE?' said Karl.

'You stick those up?' said Stu.

'No,' said Karl. 'I make a thousand pounds a week online without leaving my house. Except it's not really a thousand pounds a week. I suppose it could be if you never went to sleep.'

'So you're self-employed,' said Janna. 'But what's the work?'

'Search engine evaluation, product reviews,' said Karl. 'Literature essays for rich students. It's actually duller than it sounds.'

'A fellow middle-class underachiever,' said Stu.

'You know the type.'

'I *was* the type. Look, you don't need to rush into anything, but this is a chance to do something with your life. The Transition isn't a punishment, it's an opportunity.'

He took two thick, stapled forms out of his shoulder bag and a blue pen.

'You'll be living with us as equals – we eat together, talk together, leave the house for work together. Or, well, Karl, in your case you'll be staying in the house to work, but you get the point.'

Genevieve and Karl, who had never read a contract in their lives, both turned to the final page of their forms, wrote their names in block capitals, signed.

'The thing is, with the hair, it's a lightning conductor,' said Stu. 'People think, *Oh, the guy with the hair.* Or they think, *In spite of the hair, he's quite a nice guy.* Any opinion that anyone ever holds about me is in the context of my hair. It's the equivalent of being a beautiful woman.'

'To be fair it *is* the most interesting thing about him,' said Janna, giving Stu a friendly but very hard punch on the shoulder, which he rubbed, pouting. 'The removal team are picking up your stuff now, so that's taken care of. We'll see you for the general meeting in the morning, okay?'

Stu folded up their contracts and slipped them back into his shoulder bag.

'Tomorrow then,' he said. 'The Transition will send a car. Eight thirty.'

They stood.

'We want you to know that we don't judge you,' said Janna.

'Oh,' said Genevieve. 'Thanks.'

'What she means,' said Stu, 'is that we don't expect you to be grateful for this . . . situation. But we hope you'll be nicely surprised by the set-up tomorrow. We hope you have as brief, as useful and as mutually pleasant an experience as possible.'

'Okay,' said Genevieve. 'Thank you for . . . Thanks.'

'What made you sign up to this as mentors?' said Karl. 'If you don't mind my asking. What's in it for you?'

'We love this company,' said Janna. 'We're proud to work for the Transition.'

'A few years ago my generation kicked the ladder away behind us,' said Stu. 'This is our chance to teach you to free-climb.'

'Oh, God, always with the analogies,' said Janna. 'It's so embarrassing.'

'Besides which, and I'm going to be honest with you,' said Stu, 'only crazy people lie; we never wanted children –'

'We never wanted babies,' said Janna.

'Right, babies,' said Stu. 'Or children, really. Or teenagers. Plenty of our friends did and I can't say it appealed.'

'But sometimes we'd be talking and Stu would say, "What if we'd had kids?" '

'What if we'd met each other at, say, twenty, and had kids?'

'What would they be doing now? And it just got me thinking, *What would my grown-up kids be doing now?*'

'What kind of advice would we give them?' said Stu.

'But you can't adopt a 30-year-old,' said Janna.

'Until now,' said Genevieve. 'Well, if it's the only way out of the fine mess my husband's landed us in, consider yourselves *in loco parentis.*'

And Karl was surprised to see his wife put her arms around Janna who, a little disconcerted, patted her on the back, light and rapid as if tapping out a code.

They spent the night painting over Blu-Tack stains with Tipp-Ex. Then Genevieve scrubbed the floors with a hard brush and a cartoonish bucket of soap suds and Karl asked her why she was bothering.

The next morning a black 4x4 was waiting for them outside their eviscerated flat.

The driver leaned out.

'Transition?' he said.

It felt like they were gliding over the potholed roads. It was an auto-drive, so for the most part the driver sat with his hands behind his head, watching the blue orb move up the map. Now and then he took the little steering column to fine-tune the car's decisions, or put his foot down to override its obedience so that a stern female voice said, *Speed limit exceeded.* They were driven through urban clearways and bypasses, across double roundabouts and out-of-town shopping centres which had been absorbed into the town, past the football ground.

They were entering a rougher part of town, but the high-rises had been freshly painted porcelain white. You looked at them and thought of a tropical island hotel rather than Findus Crispy Pancakes and canned cider; although Karl disliked neither, now that he thought of it.

A building site promised a forthcoming swimming pool and multi-gym.

'All that,' said the driver, 'that renovation – paid for by the Transition. I grew up around here.'

The car turned before a railway bridge and crunched over a gravel drive before entering an industrial estate. Corrugated-metal warehouses with big numbers and little signs. They passed a car mechanic, a boxing gym, a company called Rubberplasp whose name bounced around Karl's auditory centre. Further in, the lots turned hipster: a craft brewery, a Japanese pottery, a vanity recording studio. Karl expected the Transition's headquarters to be another identical shack, but when they rounded the last corner they were at the foot of a hill from which emerged four shiny black obelisks connected by footbridges, a letter H at every rotation. Each obelisk was roughly as tall as an electricity pylon, but only broad enough to contain a couple of rooms.

As they stepped out of the taxi the shiny black surface of the four towers turned blue and brightened until it almost matched the sky. A film of a flock of birds flew across it, disappearing between the towers, which faded to black again.

'This is . . .' said Karl. 'Wow.'

'Hmm,' said Genevieve.

A young woman was standing at the door of the first tower they came to. She had an earpiece which stood out against her short, fair hair. They gave their names.

'You're married – that's so sweet!' she said. 'Everyone is on the mezzanine. Floor 8. Here are your tablets.'

She gave them each what looked like a giant After Eight mint: a very thin square touch-screen computer in a protective sleeve.

'Pretty,' said Genevieve.

'I was told this was a pilot scheme,' said Karl. 'It looks . . .'

The towers went through the sky sequence again.

'Fairly well established. We've been going for eleven years,' said the woman with the earpiece. 'We try to stay under the radar.'

The lift opened on a wide balcony full of couples. Instantly shy, Karl stood to admire a giant hyperrealist painting of a pinball table, Vegas neons and chrome. He stared at the electric-pink 100 POINTS bumpers and the matte plastic of a single raised flipper. He felt Genevieve take his hand. She did this rarely.

'What a waste of a wall,' she said.

'I like it.'

'You like pinball? You like bright colours?'

'I like the painting.'

'You're such a boy. Boys love bright colours. Like bulls,' said Genevieve. 'That's why underwear is brightly coloured. Do you remember that bag I had, the one with the Tunisian tea advert with the sequins? Grown men stopped me on the street to say they liked my bag. I told Amy and she was like, what they mean is *I like your vagina.*'

Karl paused to make sure Genevieve had finished her train of thought. She had barely said a word for the last two weeks, but today she had opinions, theories; she even had analogies. It was like she had been recast. It had taken him three years of marriage to learn that it was best to let her recalibrate without too much comment. Get a little depressed, then a little high in inverse proportion. Balance the ship.

He looked at the reflection of the garish surface in the painting of the large ball bearing. It dominated the right-hand side of the canvas. It was so convincing he expected to see a reflection of his face peering into it. As you got closer you could almost make out the fine brushstrokes.

'I just think it's incredible anyone can paint something that looks so much like a photograph,' he said.

'Yeah,' said Genevieve, 'but on the other hand so fucking what, you know?'

A brushed-silver bar served free cappuccinos and muffins in three flavours: banoffee, apple and cinnamon or quadruple chocolate.

'Quadruple? I can't choose!' said Genevieve.

'Have one of each,' said the barista.

Handsome boy, thought Karl. Slightly wounded expression. An RSC bit-player face.

'*Really?*'

'Three muffins, Genevieve?' said Karl.

'Don't listen to him,' said the barista.

'I never do.'

She sounded too grateful. But then everyone Karl could see wore the glazed, winsome expression of the all clear, the last-minute reprieve. The hundred or so young couples, the other losers who had accepted the Transition in lieu of some unpayable fine or term of incarceration, looked up from checking the impressive spec of the free mint-thin laptops they'd been handed at the door to admire the sun-dappled view over the city from the 360-degree window: *Really?* And they looked at each other, too. A preponderance of attractive, well-adjusted young people of every creed and orientation. They were athletic or willowy, at worst a kind of doughy, puppy-jowled fat which spoke of donnish indolence rather than profligacy. Inconspicuously smart or very casual – torn jeans, neon T-shirts – because they were good-looking and could get away with it. The couples were casing the joint, talking to each another, making one another laugh. You wanted them as trophy friends. Thirty-somethings who could pass for teenagers.

The lights dipped gradually.

'It's getting dark,' said Genevieve.

The stage held a glossy black podium with a bar for supporting papers, a large glass screen. There were rows of designer chairs. The chairs were improbably supporting spindles of orange flesh which, when you pressed them, took a while to reshape, like a stress toy.

Karl sat down expecting to perch on an implement of torture, but it was more like a hug. As the orange pads cupped his buttocks, moulded to the small of his back and pressed his shoulder blades, he realised he was sitting in a modern classic: *Eames meets brutalism in contemporary Norway, an alien catcher's mitt.* He drafted five-star reviews in his head; it was unusual to actually experience the product first.

Genevieve sipped her coffee.

The rows filled in around them. A man sat on the corner of Karl's anorak and didn't notice, pulling Karl slightly to the right. Karl leaned towards him, then back. His coat was still trapped. He cleared his throat. He tried to make eye contact with Genevieve, who was eating her apple-and-cinnamon muffin. He leaned in again. He couldn't look at the man's face without putting himself uncomfortably close to it. He stared at the man's shoes. Brogues, a slight residue of shoe polish. He stared ahead at the empty stage. Now he had left it too long to do anything about it. If he pulled the corner of his anorak out, the man would wonder why he hadn't done so immediately. *You actually sat there for two minutes without telling me I was sitting on your coat? What's wrong with you?* Karl tensed his right shoulder and cricked his neck so that he appeared to be sitting more or less straight.

'It's Stu,' said Genevieve. 'Karl, it's Stu.'

'Yep,' said Karl, looking up to see a tall man with a Mohawk approaching the podium.

'Why is it Stu?'

'Shh.'

'Is he the boss or something?'

'Genevieve, shh.'

Stu put his hands on the lectern, cleared his throat and looked at the big glass screen which was hanging to his right, seemingly without support. It flickered and a white oblong appeared, off-centre and barely a quarter of the size of the overall screen. It was a clip-art image of a man with a briefcase taking a big step. Stu looked at the screen. Slowly the words WHAT'S STANDING BETWEEN YOU AND SUCCESS? appeared in Comic Sans by the side of the clip-art businessman. He had a perky smile, a briefcase and a wonky blue parallelogram behind him.

'What's standing between you and success?' said Stu.

Karl, to his surprise, felt disappointed. Enough that he yanked the corner of his anorak free from his neighbour, who startled. It doesn't matter how you dress it up and how good the free coffee is; the medium is the message and the medium is fucking PowerPoint. It was a dismal feeling, like the moment a delayed train is finally cancelled altogether.

But then the lights went out completely and the clip-art businessman smeared and flickered into a dance of glitches up the glass screen. Karl's knee-jerk delight at something boring going wrong was hijacked by an orchestral start via invisible speakers, and a long, low cello improvisation. As the soundtrack dissolved into electronic pops and gurgles, the image left the screen, a jagged mess of pixels, and bounced over the panoptic window, bursting into smaller copies of itself, a screensaver taking over the world; it covered the whole room, morphing into clip-art houses, clip-art office cubicles, cups of coffee, ties and cufflinks, clip-art strong, independent women, clip-art harried-looking commuters. The seats by this point were vibrating and Karl's laughter was distorted, like a child in a play-fight. The images seemed to peel off the glass and float along the rows. The room was swimming in obsolete icons and logos, slogans and mangled business speak – push the change, be the envelope – clip-art Filofaxes and aeroplanes, shoes and computers duplicating, fanning out like cards, whirling and distending, breaking into fragments. The cello piece was melodic, abrasive, fearfully attractive, and the windows resolved into operating systems and programmes Karl remembered from childhood, a museum of dead technology, single ribbons of green text, and then the music stopped, the darkness was complete until a spotlight picked out Stu, adjusting the point of the second spike of his Mohawk.

'Sorry about that,' he said. 'Bit gimmicky.'

Karl was one of the first to start clapping.

'All right, all right,' said Stu. 'There's no getting away from the fact that this is a lecture, and I know there's not a single couple in the room who's chosen to be here so you can't blame me for falling back on special effects. I don't know if you've had a chance to talk to anyone else yet?'

Silence. Aside from discussing the scene with their partner, none of the couples had exchanged more than a resigned nod, a hello which could have been a hiccup.

'You all have something in common,' Stu smirked. 'I'm kidding. It's true, though. You're all feeling a little bruised, I'm assuming. You're all here under duress, expecting to count out the minutes, endure the insult to your intelligence. You were probably expecting . . .' He rubbed his right eye. 'You were probably expecting something like a speed-awareness course, right? I know what they're like – I've been on three.' He looked at the floor in mock contrition then glanced up. A ripple of laughter. 'Well, I'm biased because I love this company, but it's more like being given a new car. Take out your tablets.'

A mass shifting in the orange chairs. Karl slipped the computer out of its fur-lined pouch. It was a sheet of black glass, eight inches square. The words HELLO, KARL! in the middle. He looked at Genevieve, who was already moving a glowing white orb around hers with her index finger.

'Your copy of the Transition handbook is on there,' said Stu. 'It has everything from the FAQs – constantly updated – and the history of the scheme to the complaints procedure, which we hope you won't be needing. But aside from that, you just write on them like a slate. Try it. Write *Hello, Stu.*'

Clusters of HELLO, STU!s appeared on the screen behind him.

'Good,' he said. 'We're going to look at three articles. Use your tablets and just write down your reactions. Whatever comes into your head. Be completely honest.'

The screen faded into a photograph and a long headline. A young woman in an old-fashioned floral-print dress posed by a spiral staircase. The headline: WHEN THIS DESIGNER'S FAMILY GREW SHE BOUGHT THE APARTMENT DOWNSTAIRS AND MADE THEIR HOME A DUPLEX. After ten seconds she was replaced by a man with a beard stirring an orange crockpot: HOW GREG'S POP-UP RESTAURANTS BECAME A PERMANENT CHAIN AND MADE HIM A PROPERTY MAGNATE. Next a shiny man who looked about twelve adjusting his tie in the mirror: WHILE PLAYING WITH HIS TWO-YEAR-OLD DAUGHTER, THIS 26-YEAR-OLD HAPPENED UPON AN IDEA WHICH REVOLUTIONISED THE WAY WE SEE PUBLIC RELATIONS OVERNIGHT. All three appeared together with their headlines.

'I remind you that this is a completely anonymous process,' said Stu. 'We're interested in your frank, knee-jerk opinions. You have ten seconds.'

Gradually the magazine clippings disappeared from the screen and a selection of comments scrolled across the glass and around the windows:

> I want to kill them all

> HOW A PRIVATE INCOME AND MASSIVE INHERITANCE MADE ALL THESE ASSHOLES' DREAMS COME TRUE!

> oh fuck off just fuck off fuck off fuck off

> seriously a designer who can make enough to buy TWO FLATS fuck you what does she design nuclear weapons?

'Good,' said Stu. 'This is all good.'

Karl watched as his own comment – *What kind of a monster would bring a child into this world?* – performed a loop-the-loop off the screen and landed on the window facing east.

'Okay,' said Stu, as the last of the two hundred comments disappeared into a spiral behind him, as if going down a plughole. 'I'd like to welcome to the stage Susannah, Greg and Paul.'

The trio walked onstage in unison, dressed exactly as they had been in the projected magazine articles. Susannah's dress, Karl noticed, actually had a Russian doll motif. They stopped in the middle of the stage and turned to face the audience, who were quiet. Karl shook his head. Genevieve had put her hand on his knee. The bearded chef folded his arms and looked up, bashfully. The designer and the PR man smiled with a hint of defiance. Karl's temples pulsed. A lone voice yelled 'BOOOO!' which caused some brief, relieved laughter, shared by those onstage.

'Susannah, out of interest, what *do* you design?' said Stu.

'Patterns for mugs and tableware,' said Susannah.

'And maybe you could tell the ladies and gentlemen of the audience what exactly you were doing two years ago today?'

'This time two years ago,' said Susannah, pointing into the crowd, 'I was sitting in that chair, that one, fourth row. I was sitting in that chair writing shitty comments about the three people onstage because they were more successful than me.'

'We know what it's like out there,' said Stu, taking the stage. 'The landlord puts the rent up every six months. We know. Let alone saving, it's hard to meet the bills and pay down your debts once you've stumped up the rent. We *know*. You never expected to be earning the salary you're earning, but on the other hand you never expected to have to think twice about whether you could afford a new pair of socks this month. You're trapped. The debts keep growing. We know. You're overqualified for everything except a job that doesn't actually exist – a historian or something. We *know*. This is the most expensive house in London.'

A moving image of a hallway covered in dust and rat droppings appeared behind Stu. The point of view moved inwards towards a grand, sweeping staircase with moss growing on it.

'Uninhabited for twelve years. A giant, house-shaped gambling chip. None of this is fair. We *know* it's not fair. There's no changing that. So what can you do? You can throw in the towel, eat cereal straight from the box, watch Internet porn and wait for death, if that's what you want. Or you can be part of the solution. You can get into a position of power and wield it with a little more responsibility. That's what this is about.' ■

Javier Zamora

Cassette-tape

A.

To cross México we're packed in boats
20 aboard, 18 hours straight to Oaxaca.
Throw up and gasoline keep us up. At 5 a.m.
we get to shore, we run to the trucks, cops
rob us down the road—without handcuffs,
our guide gets in their Fords and we know
it's all been planned. Not one peso left
so we get desperate—*Diosito, forgive us*
for hiding in trailers. We sleep in Nogales till
our third try when finally, I meet Papá Javi.

\>>.

Mamá, you left me.   Papá, you left me.
Abuelos, I left you.   Tías, I left you.
Cousins, I'm here.   Cousins, I left you.
Tías, ~~welcome.~~   Abuelos, we'll be back soon.
Mamá, let's return.   Papá ¿por qué?
Mamá, marry for papers. Papá, marry for papers.
Tías, abuelos, cousins, be careful.
I won't marry for papers. ~~I might marry for papers.~~
I won't be back soon.   I can't vote anywhere,
I will etch visas on toilet paper and throw them from a lighthouse.

<<.

When I saw the coyote—
       I didn't want to go
but parents had already paid.
       I want to pour their sweat,
each step they took,
       and braid a rope.
I want that chord
       to swing us back
to our terracotta roof. No,
       I wanted to sleep
in my parents' apartment.

B.

"You don't need more than food,
a roof, and clothes on your back."
I'd add Mom's warmth, the need
for war to stop. Too many dead
cops, too many tattooed dead.

¿Does my country need more of us
to flee with nothing but a bag?
Corrupt cops shoot "gangsters"
from armored cars. *Javiercito,*
parents say, *we'll send for you soon.*

>>.

Last night, Mom wanted to listen to "Lulu's Mother,"
    a song she plays for the baby she babysits.

I don't know why this song gets to me, she said, then:

"Ahhhh Lu-lu-lu-lu / don't you cry / Mom-ma won't go / a-way /
Ahhhh Lu-lu-lu-lu / don't you cry / Pop-pa won't go / a-way . . ."

It's mostly other nannies in the class; *it's supposed to help*
    with the babies' speech development, she says, *mijo,*

sorry for leaving. I wish I could've taken you to music classes.

She reached over, crying. Mom, you can sing to me now
    was all I could say, you can sing to me now.

TO LIVE AND DIE
IN SOUTH KOREA

Françoise Huguier

Introduction by A.M. Homes

What is the desire to touch the experience of death and live to tell the tale? Is it a kind of psychic intervention, a scared straight of the soul? You write your final words, your confession – you relieve yourself of the burdens; the anger, the shame, the unsaid everything. You crawl into a coffin and lie silent in the dark for ten minutes – surrendering to fear, grief, relief?

In South Korea suicide is the number-one cause of death among ten- to thirty-year-olds. There is what many perceive as a cultural intolerance for failure, and depression is seen as a sign of weakness.

What is suicide in that cultural context? Is it an act of self-punishment, of surrender? Before society tells you you've failed, you will take care it by of punishing yourself? Or is it a Willy Loman, an Attention-Must-Be-Paid moment?

The idea behind the treatment for depression documented in this photoessay is that if you get close to death, if you touch it in a deeply personal way, you come closer to life – i.e. blow the candle out, taste the darkness and come back changed.

Perhaps a gathering such as the one at Hyowon Healing Center can be seen as a new form of meditation practice. Yoga often ends with Savasana (Corpse Pose), a moment associated with giving up attachment to things and simply breathing.

Breath, the one thing that divides the living from the dead. ∎

GRANTA

THE MAGAZINE OF NEW WRITING

PRINT SUBSCRIPTION REPLY FORM FOR US, CANADA
AND LATIN AMERICA (includes digital and app access).
For digital-only subscriptions, please visit granta.com/subscriptions.

GUARANTEE: If I am ever dissatisfied with my *Granta* subscription, I will simply notify you, and you will send me a complete refund or credit my credit card, as applicable, for all un-mailed issues.

YOUR DETAILS

TITLE ....
NAME ....
ADDRESS ....
....
CITY... STATE ....
ZIP CODE .... COUNTRY.......................................
EMAIL ....

☐ Please check this box if you do not wish to receive special offers from *Granta*
☐ Please check this box if you do not wish to receive offers from organisations selected by *Granta*

PAYMENT DETAILS

1 year subscription: ☐ US: $48   ☐ Canada: $56   ☐ Latin America: $68

3 year subscription: ☐ US: $120   ☐ Canada: $144   ☐ Latin America: $180

Enclosed is my check for $ ⎯⎯⎯⎯⎯⎯ made payable to *Granta*.

Please charge my: ☐ Visa   ☐ MasterCard   ☐ Amex

Card No. ☐☐☐☐☐☐☐☐☐☐☐☐☐☐☐☐

Expiration date ☐☐ / ☐☐

Security Code ☐☐☐☐☐☐☐

SIGNATURE .... DATE ....

Please mail this order form with your payment instructions to:

Granta Publications
PO Box 359
Congers, NY 10920-0359

Or call 845-267-3031
Or visit GRANTA.COM/SUBSCRIPTIONS for details   Source code: BUS137PM

JAN VAN EYCK
Portrait of Giovanni Arnolfini and his wife, 1434
© National Gallery, London / Bridgeman Images

VLADIMIR IN LOVE

Lara Vapnyar

S he was tall. Taller than him. Thin. Wide hips. Long nose. None
of his friends thought she was pretty. Marik once said that Lena
was built like a kangaroo. And Kostik just hooted in agreement. But
Vladimir thought Lena resembled a large bird.

Like a heron or a crane.

They had met in the summer of 1975. Vladimir was twenty-two
and had just graduated from Leningrad State University. He came to
the sixtieth birthday party of his old karate teacher, Arkadij Isakovich.
Lena didn't really belong at the party. She was just a distant relative
of Arkadij Isakovich visiting from Moscow, sleeping on the couch in
a dark corner of the kitchen. During the party the couch was heaped
with all the food waiting for its turn on the table, so Lena had no
choice but to join Arkadij Isakovich's guests. She sat perched on the
edge of the chair at the corner of the table, refusing offers of vodka,
not smiling, staring into the mound of beet salad on her plate, as if she
wanted to hide in there. Fat and drunk Aunt Galya kept screeching
that Lena should swap places with one of the men, because it was a bad
omen if a young girl sat at the corner. 'Nobody will want to marry her!'

At some point Lena apparently had enough. She got up and said
that she was going to the kitchen 'to get more pickles'.

She rolled her r's.

Vladmir saw her in the kitchen on his way to the bathroom. She was sitting on the windowsill with her back to him, blue cotton dress, chin-length light brown hair, long legs swinging to the floor, a jar of pickles in her hands. When he came out of the bathroom, she was still sitting there.

He walked up to her and asked: 'What are you looking at?'

She blushed and said that she was nearsighted, but she thought there was a cat in the window of the adjacent building. He walked closer. The time must have been about 6 p.m., the sun was still up, but the enclosed space between the buildings was always dark. He had to press his face right to the glass in order to see anything outside. He wondered if he stank of alcohol.

'See? Over there!' she pointed, fixing a strand of light brown hair behind her ear. The skin of her neck looked very clean.

Yes, there was a cat, a large one, sitting in the sixth floor's window and staring right at them, with mean indifference.

They looked at that cat for a long time, because neither of them was brave enough to turn and face the other.

He called Arkadij Isakovich the next day and asked if he could speak to Lena. 'Vovka, why?' Arkadij Isakovich asked. Vladimir didn't say anything, just cleared his throat, then cleared his throat again – this time more assertively.

Arkadij Isakovich sighed and gave the phone to Lena.

'Yes?' she said in a very small voice.

'How long are you here for?'

'Three more weeks.'

He told her that he felt it was his duty as a Leningrad native to show her around.

She said that her mother had made a list of all the important landmarks for her. The Hermitage, the Russian Museum, Petrodvorets. 'I don't really care about art,' she said, 'but my mom would be mad if I don't go. She says I must, while I'm here.'

They decided to meet by the entrance, and Vladimir arrived twenty minutes early. He wore his best shirt, a tight one with long lapels, made in Hungary, and his very tight pants made in East Germany – he had bought all that from his friend Kostik with the money he had made on his summer construction job. He was pacing around the square, wondering if he should've brought flowers. He wanted to, but then he thought that she'd have to carry them around the museum, and that would be stupid. Then he saw her loping toward him from the tram stop, wearing the same blue dress. The skirt ended right above her knees; she had an odd-looking purse hanging on her elbow, and she was out of breath, smiling. He regretted not buying the flowers.

Once inside, they were made to wear felt slippers. 'Our floors are a work of art!' the museum guard explained. They rummaged in the huge bin of slippers trying to find the ones that would be roughly their size. Lena picked blue ones to match her dress. The slippers were supposed to be worn over shoes. They had ribbons that you had to tie around your ankles. He watched how Lena studied them, trying to figure out which ribbon went where. Her legs were covered with thin golden hairs. He was hoping that she'd ask for his help in tying the ribbons, but she didn't.

It was pretty hard to walk in those slippers. 'I feel like a duck,' Lena said. 'Don't you feel like a duck?' And Vladimir did a duck walk for her and even said: 'Krya-krya-krya' in the best duck voice he could muster. Lena laughed so hard that the guard shook a finger at her.

It was easier to glide than walk, so they glided through all those rooms, very fast, barely pausing to look, so that the paintings merged into a sort of cartoon, a flickering of images: candles, globes, silver armor, velvet dresses, breasts. He would turn away from the breasts to show Lena his modesty and respect. There must have been a lot of people in the museum, it was crowded at all times, but he didn't register anybody at all. It was as if they were alone. Lena lost her slipper on the staircase leading to the Renaissance floor, and he had to skip down a few steps to retrieve it. This time she let him tie the ribbons.

They continued their glide, until they got to the room that housed a visiting exhibition from the National Gallery in London. Lena stopped in front of one of the paintings and started giggling. The painting was called *The Arnolfini Portrait* by Jan van Eyck. The woman was pregnant and very young, wearing something that looked like heavy curtains with frills. And the man – presumably her husband – was wearing a lampshade of a hat, a fur coat and black stockings (stockings!). Vladimir thought that Lena was laughing at the clothes, so he snickered too. 'This is uncanny!' she said. 'What?' he asked. 'The resemblance! Doesn't the guy in the painting look just like you?'

The man had a long, sad face. He looked nothing like Vladimir, who was about to take offense when Lena said, 'Like this!' and reached with her hand and moved his hair away from his forehead. Her fingers were clammy and small, and so warm that it took his breath away. 'See? He has your nose and your mouth!' Vladimir caught her other hand and squeezed it in his.

After they were finished with the museum, he took her to the best ice-cream parlor in the city, where they were served ice cream in stainless-steel bowls – three perfectly round scoops smothered in syrup. Lena ate all of hers and one of his.

She asked about his studies. He said that he was top of his class in law school. She was duly impressed. She said that she hated her school – a college for Communication Engineers. Math and physics were torture. Vladimir said that he hated math too. What he loved was history, especially Soviet history, especially World War II. She said she loved psychology, even though it wasn't taught at her school. She just liked reading about it. She loved personality tests! 'Do you have a pen?' she asked. Vladimir produced a beautiful ballpoint pen with the engraving: TO DEAR VOLODYA, ON HIS SIXTEENTH BIRTHDAY. She took a piece of paper from her purse (all crumpled and stained), handed it to him and asked him to draw an animal that didn't exist in nature.

'Just imagine something, anything at all.' She turned away to give him creative freedom.

He was nervous; he had no idea what the test might reveal. He thought that the worst would be if the test showed him as boring or meek. He decided to make his drawing as wild and detailed as possible. Big too. He made sure to take up almost the entire space.

'Oy!' Lena said when he invited her to look. Then she covered her mouth and giggled.

What he had drawn was a cross between a mammoth, a wolf and a caterpillar. A fat hairy beast with sharp teeth, huge ears, sparkling eyes and many many legs.

'So?' he said.

'Well,' she started, 'you're curious about the world – I can see that because you made the eyes and ears so big. And the drawing looks kind of crazy, so you must be adventurous.'

Yes! he thought.

'You might be a little greedy, because you took so much space. Perhaps a bit insecure. Easy to hurt.'

What? he thought. No! His distress must have shown, because she smiled apologetically and touched his hand.

'I say that because none of his many legs is touching the ground. See?'

Yes, she was right. Why, why couldn't he have drawn all the legs on the same level?

'And, well, it has this huge bushy tail.'

'What does that mean?' he asked.

She blushed and murmured that she'd rather not say.

He didn't kiss her that day, or the day after when they glided through the Russian Museum. He kissed her the next weekend, when they made a trip to Petrodvorets. Lena's mother insisted that she see the interior of Petrodvorets Palace, but the line to buy tickets was inhumanely long and neither of them was particularly interested in staring at the 'tsar's night vases and stuff'. So they just walked and walked around the grounds, marveling at all that gold and marble and the brilliant gushing water of the fountains. There were hordes of people there, noisy, sweaty, pushing their way through and hoisting their kids onto their shoulders or aiming their bulky cameras. Vladimir found it funny that all those people had no idea how little they mattered. He could've blown them all up, and it wouldn't have changed anything. As long as Lena was there.

The best thing in Petrodvorets was the trick fountains. The spigots there were concealed in various innocent objects, and would erupt and shoot water at people at random moments, when they least expected it. Vladimir took Lena's hand and they were running in and running out, jumping over the jets, crossing the invisible lines, trying to out-trick the trick fountains, screaming and laughing, until they got soaked through and had to retreat to a bench, where they sat down, out of breath and shivering.

Her face was wet and cold and her mouth was slippery but her body breathing at him through the damp folds of her dress was burning hot and her heart was beating like crazy.

After that trip, they found that the cultural riches of Leningrad didn't interest them anymore and they preferred to meet in remote corners of the city's parks, or dark staircases of random buildings, and sometimes they would even take a tram and ride all the way to its last stop and back, kissing the entire way.

Two weeks later, Vladimir's parents went to their dacha and Vladimir asked Lena to his place. The apartment was very neat, but Vladimir dusted it one more time, and polished the already spotless floor. Then he took a tram to the center, went to the Nord bakery – the best one in the city – and bought his favorite cake, the layered one, glazed with chocolate and covered with walnuts. It was called Leningrad. At home, he put the cake in the fridge, bathed and shaved, spraying himself generously with the eau de cologne Shipr Korolevskiy – he had bought the bottle from Kostik a year ago, but had never used it because it was so expensive. He should've bought flowers, but now it was too late. Lena was due to appear at any moment.

'Do you want cake?' was the first thing he asked her, when he opened the door for her.

Lena shook her head. She was distant and quiet and her eyes had a panicked expression. She wore a short-sleeved blouse already darkened under the arms, bringing a complicated bouquet of female smells.

He took her on a tour of the apartment, which was just two rooms. 'This is my room,' he said, 'This is my desk. These are my books. Do you like history?'

'Not really,' Lena said, but walked closer to the shelves. 'Oh, that's adorable!' she cried, pointing to a framed photo of Vladimir at the age of twelve. Side bangs and shy smile. He blushed and said that it was his mom who put it there. They talked about their parents a bit. Lena said that if she had to describe her parents in one word, she would choose 'disgruntled'. They behaved as if they had been cheated of something very important in their lives. Vladimir said that he would choose the word 'old'.

'Oy! What's that?' she asked, pointing at another framed photograph of a very handsome man in Nazi uniform.

'That's Alexander Belov from the *The Shield and the Sword*. The Russian intelligence officer posing as a Nazi.'

'*The Shield and the Sword*?' she asked.

'I can't believe you don't know it. It's my favorite film.'

She shrugged apologetically.

'So here is what happens in the movie,' he said. 'Belov is a Soviet officer who learns German and goes to Germany right before the war, so he can infiltrate the German forces. And he is really clever, so he manages to build a great career over there in just a year or two. The Nazis send him to work in a concentration camp, Auschwitz, I think. They put him in charge of the spy school.'

'There was a spy school there?'

'There is in the movie. The Germans came up with the idea of training Russian prisoners to become German spies. They would break their spirit first, so they would agree to serve the enemy. Then they would teach the men how to operate a radio and make technical drawings, and they would teach the women how to operate a radio and be prostitutes.'

He blushed and cleared his throat when he said 'prostitutes'. Then he continued, 'When the students were ready, they would send them to Russia – drop them off planes with parachutes. They were supposed to spend some time there, gather the needed information and send it back to Germany.'

Vladimir saw that Lena's eyes had glazed over a little. It wasn't easy to hold her attention, so he had to try harder.

'But when they put Belov in charge of the school, he subverted the entire operation. You see, he would reveal to the smartest and the most reliable students that he was in fact a Soviet intelligence officer, and together they could do a great service to the Motherland. So what they did was sabotage the missions and even send false information to Germany.'

'Uh-huh,' Lena said.

'But imagine how hard his life must have been! Not to have any contact with your family, to pretend to be somebody else every second of every day, to live among the enemy, to pretend to make friends with the vile swine.'

'That's really tough, yeah,' Lena said. 'You have to be really smart to do it, and patient too.'

'That's what I want to do.'

'To be a spy?'

'No! An intelligence officer!'

'Really?' she asked.

'I love the theme song from that movie – you must know it.'

She shook her head.

He cleared his throat and sang the first line: 'What is the seed of the Motherland . . .'

'Oh, yes!' she said. 'Of course, I know that song! I love that song. I just didn't know it was from a movie.' And she sang in a faltering voice, rolling her r's:

What is the seed of the Motherland?
A picture in your spelling book.
The friends that you've known as children,
Their homes half a block away . . .

He caught her face in his hands and kissed her on the mouth. Then he picked her up and carried her to the sofa.

They spent about two hours on that sofa (blue balls hurting like hell), before she relaxed enough to let him slip two fingers inside her panties.

'I'm a virgin,' she whispered.

'Do you want me to stop?' he asked.

'No, I just think that we should put a towel underneath. In case there is blood.'

He ran to the bathroom to get a towel, picking one his mother wouldn't miss.

When he got back, she was naked, lying on her side, facing the wall. He spread the towel right under her butt. Then he took off his clothes, put a condom on and lay down next to her.

'I'll be gentle,' he said into her back.

'Please, don't,' she whispered. 'My friends tell me that it hurts less if a boy is forceful and quick.'

Then she turned onto her back and spread her legs, trusting him to hurt her.

When he did, she cried out in pain and he wondered whether he should stop or continue. He was done before he could make a decision. He rolled off and kissed her on the cheek.

There was a huge smile of relief on her face.

'I'm a woman now!' she said. 'Just like that. I can't believe it!'

'Yes,' he said, 'and I am your first man.'

'Yes, you are!'

She went to wash herself and rinse the bloody towel. Then he went to wash.

'Let's have that cake now,' she said. 'Can we have it in your room?'

He nodded, even though his mother didn't usually allow him to eat in his room, put on his pants and went to the kitchen.

'Do you have any milk?' she yelled after him.

He cut two large slices, put them on the good plates, poured milk into the good glasses, put it all on a tray and brought it to his room.

He had expected her to get dressed while he was in the kitchen, but found her sitting cross-legged on the sleeper sofa, naked.

'Such a beautiful cake!' she said, taking the plate with a crumbly slice of Leningrad. 'And delicious too,' she added with her mouth full.

Her small breasts drooped toward her stomach, which gathered into little folds like an accordion, her armpit hair was long and damp, and her wild bush was too close to the plate with the cake. Vladimir found all of this immodest and unhygienic, but she looked so happy and was clearly enjoying herself so much that he couldn't help but forgive her.

When she asked for seconds, he said that he wouldn't mind seconds too and winked at her, but she smiled and shook her head and said that she needed to heal first.

It had gotten dark. He suggested they go to his parents' room to watch TV. She put on her clothes – bra, panties, the blouse, the wrinkled skirt. He brought them more cake, put it on the table and crouched in front of the TV so he could turn the knob that flipped channels. Not that there were many channels.

He prayed that there would be something good to watch, and found that they were in luck – the rerun of his favorite series, *Seventeen Moments of Spring*, was about to start!

'*Seventeen Moments!*' Lena cried. 'Yes!'

He picked up his plate and snuggled next to her.

They had been eating all through the titles, but as soon as the first scene started she put her plate down.

'This is my favorite scene,' she whispered.

In that scene, Max Otto von Stierlitz, an SS Standartenführer (but really Soviet intelligence officer Maxim Isaev), is walking in the bare deserted woods. At some point, he raises his head and watches a flock of cranes move slowly across the sky. He looks tough, but sad, clearly tired of pretending to be a Nazi. A melancholy theme song is playing in the background, brazenly sentimental, brutally tearful.

'Do you know what he is thinking right now?' Lena asked.

'What?'

'He envies the cranes. They are free, and he is stuck there with the Nazis. He wishes he could become a crane and fly away with them. But he can't.'

There were tears in her eyes.

Could it be that I love her? Vladimir thought.

Years later, when the president of Russia, Vladimir Putin, announced that he would lead a flock of cranes by flying with them in a motorized hang glider, people asked what inspired him to do it. He would give many answers, but never the true one.

O ther people in Vladimir's life started noticing that something was up.

First, his mother inquired how the guest towel ended up on the rack in the bathroom.

Then, his friend Marik asked if Vladimir was still seeing that girl from the party. Vladimir confirmed that he was. 'Why?' Marik said, 'She's not even pretty and she's built like a kangaroo.'

Then it was Arkadij Isakovich's turn.

'No, Vovka, no!' he said. 'Trust me, you don't want to get mixed up with that family. You've had your fun, but that's it. You have a brilliant future ahead of you. Don't let her derail that.'

And he knew that Arkadij Isakovich was right. She was a Jew. That was not good. The times were different now, but still, being a Jew or having a Jewish wife was never good.

Well, he thought, she would leave for Moscow in a few days anyway. And that was what they needed. Some time apart. Some time to cool off.

On their last evening together, they were walking down the dark city streets. It was a cool night. Lena was shivering. She was clinging to him. He wished he had a jacket on so he could take it off and drape it over her shoulders. It was time to take her back to Arkadij Isakovich's place. They had to take a tram, but there were none in sight. They sat down on the bench in the glassed-in booth. There was a poster for yet another new thriller hanging behind them. Three Soviet intelligence officers in felt hats stared at them from the poster.

Vladimir took Lena's hand and they sat in silence for some time. Then she looked at him and said: 'Vova.'

There was so much affection in her voice that it made him choke.

'Lena, let's get married,' he said, surprising himself.

She opened her mouth to say something, but he wouldn't let her.

'Listen, just listen,' he said. 'I'm joining the KGB in the fall. I've been selected. That's a big honor. And don't worry. It doesn't matter that you're a Jew, the times are different now. I don't think they would kick me out just because I'm marrying a Jew. I would need to do some training, but after that the possibilities are endless. It's a really good job. We will buy a car. They promised me an apartment within a few years. We will have our own apartment! You will have imported clothes. Special food rations. Salami, caviar. I could even get a foreign assignment. How does Germany sound?'

She opened her mouth again, but he wouldn't let her speak. There was something desperate in her expression, something painful, something not right. She wasn't going to say yes. It was clear. He had the sense that as soon as he let her speak, everything would be over. So he continued to talk.

'We will live at my place for a while. Then they will give me an apartment. They promised. In just a couple of years. And a car. They promised me a car, too.'

He was repeating himself. He had to stop.

'Vova,' she said. 'I can't.'

'You don't have to decide right now,' he said. 'Please, don't decide right now. Go back to Moscow tomorrow. Talk to your parents. How many years do you have left at your college? Two? You can transfer to a college here.'

'Vova, no. I can't. We are leaving. My parents and I. We are going
to Israel.'

Then she started to cry.

'When?' he asked.

'Very soon. All of the documents are ready,' she was saying
through tears and snot. 'They sent me to Leningrad because it's
been crazy at home. Mom and Dad have been arguing all the time,
screaming at each other, screaming at me.'

'Why do they want to leave?'

'I don't know how to explain. My parents say that they are wasting
their lives here. They've been waiting for this for years. They have
gone through hell to get the exit visas.'

Fucking traitors of the Motherland! he thought.

'I didn't even want to go.'

'Stay!'

'I can't. I can't do it to them. I'm all they have.'

He turned away from her and pressed the knuckles of his hands
to his forehead. He felt as if she had punched him. Right in the solar
plexus. It had happened to him in his karate class. It was worse this
time, much worse.

'When were you planning to tell me?'

'Today. Tonight. Vova, please try to understand,' and she reached
to stroke his face, but he jerked away from her.

So she had known this all along? She had known she was leaving.
He had to ask her something. Something very important. It was hard
to breathe.

'Why? Why did you? Why did you start it with me then?'

Her crying turned into sobs now, and she was speaking to him
through hiccups.

'I don't know. I liked you. I didn't expect it to be so serious.'

'Then why . . . why did you . . . why did you . . .' (He wanted to
say, 'Why did you let me fuck you' but found himself unable to say
'fuck' to her face). 'Why did you let it happen, if you didn't expect it
to be serious?'

She turned away from him. She didn't have a handkerchief, so she wiped her nose with the sleeve of her blouse.

There was something really ugly, really hateful about her, both hateful and pathetic. He wanted to hit her and he wanted to cry with her at the same time. He jumped off the bench and stared down at her.

'You didn't want to go to Israel a virgin, is that it? You wanted me to do the job, so that Jewish guys had it easy?'

She looked at him in disbelief, then stood up. It was crazy how tall she was. Her face was puffy and inexplicably ugly.

He was blocking her way.

'Let me go,' she said.

He didn't move.

She pushed him aside and started to run.

The actors from the movie poster were staring at him. Mocking him from under their felt hats.

Fucking spies! he thought, and punched the guy in the center right in his stupid face.

At 9.30 a.m., the Moscow train station in Leningrad was teeming with people standing, walking, running. Stupid, senseless people with bulky suitcases and screaming kids. It was hot and it smelled like sweat, urine and unwashed clothes. Lena's train was departing at 10.30 a.m. (Vladimir had asked Arkadij Isakovich to look at her ticket).

Vladimir arrived early, because he wasn't sure what he would do once there. He knew that he wanted to see Lena one more time, but he wasn't sure if he wanted her to see him or not. He looked up at the yellow building of the station and remembered an amusing fact he'd learned in school. The buildings of the Moscow Station in Leningrad and the Leningrad Station in Moscow were exactly the same. Identical buildings in two different cities. What an idiotic idea!

His hand hurt. He had broken the glass when he punched that poster and there were cuts so deep that it took a while for the bleeding to stop. 'Did you get into a fight again?' his mother asked while she was dressing his wound. 'Is this about a girl?'

The ice-cream kiosk was open. Vladimir walked over and bought himself an Eskimo pie. It was sweet and cold and it made his teeth hurt, but still he finished it too soon. He threw the wrapper and the stick into the garbage can and looked at the clock. It was ten – time to go the platform. He passed two Georgian men selling flowers. He asked for the red tulips – they tried to cheat him out of twenty kopeks, but he caught them in time.

The train to Moscow was already there, dusty and green and smelling of machine oil. He walked to the center of the platform and hid behind the thick column.

He stood there for twenty minutes or so, leaning against the cold marble. Peeking at the passersby like a spy. He looked at his bound hand and thought, A wounded spy. He noticed that the tulips were already starting to wilt, must have been old – those Georgians had cheated him after all. He was thirsty and he wanted to pee.

Then he saw Lena making her way down the platform, wearing that same blue dress she wore when they met. She was bent under the weight of the large leather suitcase.

His impulse was to rush over and help her carry it, but he stepped back instead.

She walked to the door of her car, put the suitcase down, handed the ticket to the conductor. While the conductor checked her ticket, Lena took a look around as if searching for him. She seemed to be looking in his direction, so he took one more step back, then remembered that she was nearsighted and couldn't see him anyway.

His heart was beating very fast and his hand squeezing the flowers was clammy with sweat.

The conductor gave Lena her ticket and she hoisted her suitcase up the steps, then climbed up herself. Her seat was in compartment 4. Vladimir counted which window that would be; the blinds were drawn. He waited for Lena to pull them up, to look out of the window, but the blinds remained closed.

The train budged and inched forward. Lena's car was creeping away from him. Then, as if by a miracle, Lena appeared at the door. She was holding on to the handle, with one long leg on the step, and the other hidden behind her, craning her neck to see the platform better. The train started to gain speed.

He wanted to rush toward her, to run after the train, to scream her name, but he remained standing there as if frozen, squeezing his tulips.

When the train was out of sight, he dropped the tulips on the floor of the platform and headed back toward the station.

> What is the seed of the Motherland?
> A picture in your spelling book.
> The friends that you've known as children,
> Their homes half a block away . . .
> Or, maybe, the seed of the Motherland
> Is the lullaby your mother sang,
> The memories stronger than trials
> That cannot be taken away. ∎

Vladimir Putin sits in a motorized hang glider next to a Siberian crane
Yamal Peninsula, September 2012

from *White Monks: A Life in Shadows*, 2009

MY ANGEL

Adam Thorpe

He woke from the dream with the wings still whirring in his ears. He was in his cell, the woollen blanket half tumbled onto the rug. He lay very still in the darkness. The stove had gone out, but the bells had not yet rung. Two o'clock? Two thirty?

The last part of the dream was still vivid in his head. They were in the fields for their weekly walk, gazing upon the flat majesty of the fens in complete silence. The walk was the one time in the week that they could freely natter to each other, but here, in the world of dreams, there was some sort of vocal interdiction. They were returning by way of the great cross beyond the east-facing walls: some twenty feet high, its weathered oak beams bearing a modest bronze Christ, it was visible for miles around. The day was cloudless, the light sharp. They were all in full white habits, hoods up, as they usually were when out walking on a cool Sunday afternoon. Then all of a sudden their cowls began rippling and shaking and lifting, until they were billowing out like laundry on a line, each brother attempting to press the unruly cloth to his thighs.

Where were the fierce gusts coming from? The distant poplars and alders were unmoved, breathlessly still; the corn in the field likewise.

They looked up at the sky together, as if at a signal.

The black dot of a lark.

Then something bigger, probably a buzzard. Then, impossibly, a swan, with huge sun-gilded wings. But it wasn't a swan, of course. The neck wasn't long enough. And where the swan's head should be was a girl's face, maybe even a young woman's   at any rate, of an unearthly gentleness and beauty but at the same time completely individual. He could somehow see this in the shifting viewpoint of the dream. The wind came from the wings; they beat in a blur, much like the wings of the mayflies darting along the creeks or over the rain barrel in the monastery's vegetable garden.

The wings slowed. She was descending towards them feet first, like a hang-glider pilot ready to land. She had a small, freckled nose. Then she tucked the wings right behind her, only to spread them out again wide and make a graceful landing on the very apex of the cross. There was a loud click, a shiver and a shake, then she gave them all a slightly toothy, utterly endearing grin, turned her head to the left and soared away with – to his great surprise – the monumental burden swinging beneath her feet like some outsize prey dangling from an eagle's claws (the bronze Christ looking a little bemused), and leaving a small hole the size of a mouse (absurd, but this was a dream). The monks' cries turned into a discussion about the technical aspects of the visitation, about speed and velocity, about the very powerful grip of an angel's toes and so on, during which gentle-mannered Brother John lost his cool with Brother William and began shouting. This woke the sleeper up, possibly with a yelp.

He could remember every detail of the dream, as though it had just happened for real.

If it actually had been a dream. He recovered the blanket and pulled the soft weave up to his chin. Apart from the arguing episode and the size of the hole, the dream was not very dreamlike, it lacked a certain surrealism. An angel plucking out the cross wasn't that crazy, in the end. It didn't feel crazy, anyway. It was like a message. A vision. Maybe he had just experienced his first vision as a monk. Monastic history was strewn with visions. They were, in some ways, what kept the whole show on the road.

Sleep was out of the question. He relit the stove and prayed in his cell, asking God what had He meant by it.

He didn't really ask, as such, he just sort of stood near Him, trying to catch His eye, loitering in the vicinity of His munificence, as it were. Wondering whether, um . . . ?

The Indivisible One, awake at all hours. No answer came before the bells. A blank. Not even a hint on the breeze, the warm ethereal breeze that sometimes brushed his cheek when he was praying, a gust of warmth in the general condition of cold breathed out by the stones and absorbed by the newer brick. The wood-burning stoves in the cells, despite being the latest thing from Denmark, struggled to make their mark: the ration of wood was too small. The rest of the monastery had no heating at all. Gradually, over time, his thermostat adjusted, but never quite enough.

What hadn't adjusted was his sight; the low light and lots more reading had ushered him into myopia. Seeing through a glass darkly. He now wore small round spectacles, Lennon-like, which had apparently come back into fashion.

He had a lot to learn. Even after four years he still felt the novice, although he was now wearing the black scapular of the professed, with its comforting, pointed hood. Next month he would be fifty. He had started late. In just over a year's time his probation would be over and he would pronounce his solemn and perpetual vows.

He briefly considered requesting a private conference with Father Jeremy. Working hard in the vegetable garden, chopping wood, sawing, stirring fudge, he felt the vision loosen a little from his mind. He took his usual nap at midday, limbs aching from the physical toil. Getting up at 3.15 in the morning, despite going to bed at eight in the evening, still took its toll on his circadian rhythms. Back in his old life – so distant now – he had felt groggy and charged simultaneously: no rhythms whatsoever, just a sluice of adrenaline.

He now reckoned the dream was not a vision after all, but the result of poor digestion. He had spent the first year here in a state of chronic hunger. Eating breakfast in what was effectively the middle of the night had been the primary challenge, but he was soon craving the granola lumped in the chunky stoneware bowl with its flawed glazes like encrustations of past meals (the best work from the abbey's pottery studio being reserved for the shop). He would seize his birchwood spoon and scoop the stuff too eagerly, and there was never enough. When, every other day, a fresh loaf appeared on the platter before him, still warm, it was all he could do to resist grabbing the bread knife before anyone else. Old Brother Felix, quietly going gaga, would cut his slice far too thick, but no one said anything. Sometimes only the heel was left. He didn't even balk at those dishes that were more revolting than the usual fare: tinned tuna with overboiled gnocchi; undercooked tofu with dank broccoli spears.

Following a session of counselling from Father Jeremy in his second year ('Try not to look forward, Brother, so much as within!'), he saw his continual conversation with the Almighty as a supreme comfort, and his holy space of a cell as the most incredible luxury, and his time here as the most extraordinary freedom, the freedom to pray for the world and all its various trials and agonies. Against these, he agreed, his previous life had been a deep and selfish impoverishment, especially after his marriage had begun to disintegrate. But he didn't mention the latter, not ever. They were not supposed to dwell on the past.

He took the hardest vow of all, eventually. The vow of stability. This being the vow to remain in this one place forever, or at least until his physical body became a nest for worms in the monks' cemetery. He had never felt more at peace. The overlarge church, where he spent many of his waking hours singing and praying, became the hub to each slowly turning day. At first, as a white-robed novitiate, he had always stood taut and still during the ragged, almost casual chanting ('We are not performing,' a sermon reminded him), and bowed very low at the end. Now, of course, he swayed or fiddled or wiped his nose or put a hand on the pew like everyone else, and his bow was undemonstrative. He even yawned, sometimes. He was normal again, but in a different world of normality. A parallel world.

After the angel dream, which had gradually lost its vivid lustre, like a pebble taken out of a stream, he took to eating his meals slowly, cherishing them and thanking God for each mouthful. He had no more night disturbances, which was proof of his original digestive supposition. He went into the garden to dig or plant or weed, or into the kitchens to scrub pots or help with the cooking or unload the antique dishwasher in the scullery, even when he'd have preferred to read by the stove or browse the leather-spined volumes in the large library or practise his mortise and tenon joints in the carpentry shop. Sometimes you don't have to seek beyond the ordinary to find an answer, he thought, watching a worm wriggle in his hand, its little body surprisingly chill from the frosty earth.

A bulky brown envelope came a week after his fiftieth – a day which otherwise went unremarked: Australian stamp, address in his daughter Jessica's handwriting. Home-made cards, hastily done with cheap felt pens. Photos, drawings. They were loving Australia. No card or letter from their mother. It all felt as distant as the dream now did.

It was never meant for him; none of it.

When, the next morning, he saw from the vegetable garden a trio of uniformed policemen talking to the prior at the main gate, he believed they were there for him: coming to take him into custody for emotional neglect, the evidence recovered from among the flattened cardboard boxes and paper wrappings. But it was about some missing teenage girl from Lincoln. In case she turned up, seeking shelter among the celibate men! He tried to avoid the newspapers, these days.

Had they all simply run away, like her, in the end?

'She looks a right canny lass,' reported Prior Christian, who hailed from Middlesbrough, where he had worked with the jobless, and was plain-speaking in a slightly self-conscious way. 'I fear the worst, I do. I told 'em we'd remember her in our prayers.'

Spring came, and with it daylight at lauds: the distant salt marsh visible from his second-floor window glittered on his return from tierce, and the cloisters' lawn was full of crocuses. Wood anemones and celandines scattered themselves about the brothers' feet on the weekly sorties, their voices and laughter bouncing back at them. It was always a surprise, when they gathered at the gate for their outing, to find their voices still worked above a murmur. It would sound, at first, as if everyone was shouting: WE LIVE IN SILENCE nailed to the gate behind like a reproof.

A minute of laughter, Brother William had read somewhere, is equivalent to a ten-mile hike. Since Brother William was both fat and ribald (his nickname was 'Tuck'), this led to many quips and yet more laughter. They must all have run a marathon, by the end. Never had he felt such joy.

He had made great progress with the food question, too. He no longer probed his plump wooden fork with his tongue for the last morsel, or scraped the annoyingly rough bowl. When a lay brother brought a fresh jug of water, he ignored his thirst and denied himself a second cup, or at least until the others had served themselves; and even then, if it had been drained unthinkingly, he would avoid peering into the jug in an obvious fashion. These days, eating in the company of his fellows, the clatter of utensils and the odd stomach rumble being the only sounds, he would strive for compassion: nevertheless, he caught himself judging the others (Brother Edmund, for instance – who ate like a pig, although he was cadaverously thin and had a small, pursed mouth). This was how the dream had made him purer in heart, whatever its source. He would even refrain, after washing in the chill stone basin along the refectory corridor, from drying his fingers on the roller towel, leaving it slightly less damp and soiled for the others.

One wet and grisly afternoon just before vespers, feeling depressed and confused, he decided to adapt the *Sortes Vergilianae* method of divination and opened his Bible at random. His finger fell upon a verse in Ecclesiastes: 'Better is one handful of quietness, than two hands full and a striving after wind.'

Inner quietness, of course, was what he must work towards. He had been reading the letters of Guigo the Angelic, written from

La Grande Chartreuse in 1150 (improving his schoolboy Latin with a bilingual edition). '*Scala claustralium qua de terra in coelum sublevantur.*' Climbing the four rungs of the immensely tall ladder to heaven: the reading of Scripture, meditation, then prayer, and up to the quiet ecstasy of contemplation. Sipping the sweet wine of the Godhead at last.

Thank you, Lord.

That being said, he couldn't help acting the architectural engineer now and again, noticing incipient problems – cracks, damp, dry rot. The original abbey building dated from the fifteenth century, although its various vicissitudes and conversions since the dissolution of the monasteries had made it unrecognisable as such: it was now more like an eighteenth-century manor with Victorian additions and a grotesque flat-roofed extension from 1984. 'Concrete savagery,' he murmured, quoting Nikolaus Pevsner, and began a subtle campaign to have it demolished.

This was no great challenge: the then-abbot had felt the place needed a modern touch and had hired a young up-and-coming architect of the brutalist school when brutalism was already fading, raising not quite enough money to use decent materials. It leaked, it was crumbling, there was an asbestos question. The day came in his second year when the asbestos had to be dealt with, and it was decided to take Brother Gideon's advice and demolish the lot. The architect (a local bigwig, vaguely known to him in his former life and studiously avoided at the time) fussed and protested, but the man was on his own.

The roof on the chapter house having to be replaced, the two jobs were done in the same three-month period in 2010. He converted the banging and crashing into a celebration, as though heavenly drums and cymbals were in action. It was a tall order, but it helped. In his old life he would have worn earplugs, as he had always been sensitive to noise, and his job had involved much smashing and stripping and knocking down, before the company itself collapsed during the Great

Crash along with his own mistaken existence. Brother Vincent from Cameroon likened it to drums from the bush, and actually swayed about in imitation of the native dancers. Animist rituals. Pagan rites. Brother Gideon smiled, feeling benign and open minded. Perhaps one day he would go out to the brother house in Cameroon and help in the clinic, get some tropical disease and die quietly in the service of others. But not for a while. He was still adjusting, still getting used to the freedom of having so few ties and worries.

The noise ceased to general relief, but as Father Jeremy had commented: 'Only in heaven are improvements and repairs and demolitions unnecessary.' How can we have buildings without noise? Brother Saul suggested they turn the muddy site into an authentic medieval herb garden with explanatory notices for visitors: they toiled, they rejoiced, they blistered their hands sunk in a sweet stink of horse dung. If the result was not yet mature, lacking pungency and atmosphere, their visitor numbers had risen steadily until a week of unstoppable deluge had washed half of it away and made the main track a glutinous mess.

As Prior Christian would say, after another defeat for Middlesbrough FC, 'The Almighty has His reasons, working in the context of eternity.'

One evening he sat at his desk and reread the scrawled account of the dream, now a few months old. In the margin he wrote, neatly, as if to dictation: 'I am full of unreal desires and worthless imaginings.' He liked the magisterial sound of that.

You could see the cross from certain windows, thrusting itself into the sky, appearing to sway against those swift clouds. Pigeons tended to use it as an alternative resting place to the monastery's finials and broad sills. The odd large crow would flap onto the pinnacle or strut up and down the outflung arms, which reminded him of paintings by Bruegel. If anything, the oversize rood had a certain vulgarity about it, a showiness that wasn't really them. It was erected in the 1930s and was very much of its period, its bronze Christ somewhat art deco with a sprout of ribbons on the side of the chest that looked like a medal but was meant to indicate the wound of the Holy Lance. A 1960s cross would have been worse, however: all in stained, crumbling concrete with horrible jutting angles and a pseudo-abstract Saviour with a face like a lobster or Darth Vader. He enjoyed imagining it, and sketched a design before he realised what he was doing and scrumpled up the paper.

It was winter again, with the odd flurry of snow, the refectory seeming not much warmer than outside. He liked feeding the pigs in the pig house, not only because he liked their white-lashed, grinning intelligence, but because it was cosy and warm.

The long track to the monastery was still in dreadful condition. Pending repairs, complicated by the fact that only part of the track was their property, they'd had to close the abbey shop and shift its fudge, rosaries, books, CDs, pottery and other quality wares to a few borrowed shelves in a village gift store several miles away. Another drop in income, although the online sales service on the website (ourladyofgraceabbey.co.uk) was almost ready.

At least this meant that the envelope of silence was torn less often by noisy visitors – cars with booming sound systems, unsupervised children like flocks of gulls, or the long fleet of German bikers that had descended in the summer: 'Angels, but we are coming from hell,' as their leader joked to Brother Vincent, manfully grinning behind the counter. Retreatants were quieter, as quietude was precisely what they were seeking: lodged in the guest house from where they emerged in bobble hats and wellies to walk the grounds or sit untidily (their hair, the civvy dress) in the abbey church, they occasionally shared a few words with him. He felt sorry for them. They had a week or two, he had the rest of his life. The monastery, like other patches of rural Lincolnshire, had no mobile signal; you had to walk several hundred yards up a muddy footpath to a slight rise near a vast field of cabbages, and lift your phone above head height. By the end of a week they were no longer bothering.

*

One day in late April, halfway round their usual route, reaching the meadow that had once been a boggy fen and was now technically dry, Father Jeremy held up his hand and they all came to a halt. This drained acreage was a 'carr', they had learned, just as a vegetated sand dune was called a 'meol'. Brother Gideon had grown to like Lincolnshire, or the small patch of it that he now resided in every day of the week and which he barely left except for medical needs. He liked the way the air, with its hints of brine and seawrack and fenland hedgerows, cooled his close-shaven pate after the itchiness of the hood. The flatness happily fulfilled the Order of Cistercians of the Strict Observance's original emphasis on the austerity of their surroundings: they might have been in Normandy in the truly ascetic days of freezing dormitories, total silence and six-month fasts. So much sky, it was suggested, drew one's thoughts towards the infinite.

The carr was full of pollarded alders, their thick stems hazed with newly budded leaves. The ground either side of the path was full of tightly knit little flowers and ferns – lady ferns and broad buckler ferns according to Brother Saul, the plant expert, who looked nineteen in his accidentally hipster specs (heavy, black) but was in his late thirties. It was all part of a protected area, of course. The soil was sandy further on, where there was a stretch of wild heath; in the summer they would lie there in the sun amidst the sweet cascades of broom (he'd thought it was gorse), exploding their seedpods: he would always nod off, of course, deliciously swirled away and returned. Heaven will be this!

Father Jeremy said he had an announcement to make. He would often make announcements during their weekly excursion out of doors: his voice was a strong, clear baritone, which went with his broad shoulders and hairy wrists, and which made any pronouncement of his deeply impressive (he was also fearsomely intelligent and well read – Cambridge professor at twenty-six, now world authority on St Jerome). He reported that a part of the great cross – one of the iron angles that acted as brace to the crosspiece – had been found on the ground. The cross was erected at a difficult time for the monks. Brother Gideon had never enquired further, but he knew it had involved a nearby school for young Catholic delinquents set up by the abbey in the 1890s and which had provoked all sorts of 'problems'. It was finally closed down in the 1950s, the brother on the staff taken on by St Bartholomew's Grammar, an excellent school which was expanding.

'What was the problem, exactly?'

'Just don't go there,' Brother Simeon advised with an unattractive simper.

The cross was a statement of confidence, or maybe defiance, funded by sympathisers in Ireland and America.

Brother Odilo (formerly Jeff, and now the abbey's highly practical cellarer) had taken a ladder and examined the cross the day before yesterday: urgent measures must be taken. The two oak timbers were not rotten or split by frost, for they were as hard as stone: they had come from a medieval tithe barn, apparently. The iron braces, however, had rusted in the salt air and the Saviour was loose. 'The restoration requires the skills of a blacksmith,' Father Jeremy declared with the same authority as when he talked of personal transformation or the still small voice of God's compassion. The one in the nearby village who usually did their metal bits had now retired, his smithy converted to a jewellery workshop. A man called Jim had been recommended.

'He also does woodwork, I'm told,' concluded Father Jeremy, 'and lives near Lincoln.'

'As people generally do,' joked Brother Simeon, who was once a footman at Buckingham Palace. He had (or so he claimed) discerned his vocation while opening a door for Prince Andrew.

The cross had to be taken to the smithy, where it would be laid horizontally and mended. But how to carry the cross, as it were? The crosspiece was very wide and the whole thing weighed tons, Father Jeremy explained. Given the state of the track, 'there's really no way your average lorry would make it through'.

'The mountain could come to Muhammad,' suggested Prior Christian, who was always as ready with a quip as Brother Simeon.

'Ideally, yes, but in reality no. In this case, believe it or not, it would be financially less painful to take it to him than for him to do lots of toing and froing. At any rate, it has to be taken out of its concrete bed and laid flat. This would involve the hire of a special and truly ginormous crane. Getting the crane here, given the present state of the track, would be impossible until the summer. The repairs are urgent.'

He turned to Brother Odilo, who said, 'Urgent is an understatement. One good easterly gale, of the type we've been suffering of late, and the crosspiece will fly off, along with Our Lord. Or at least drop off.'

'So,' Father Jeremy resumed, 'assuming Our Lord does not fancy flying off, what are we to do?'

There was a pause after a polite collective chuckle. Father Jeremy's head was lowered and his hands folded over his stomach, as if he was in deep thought. The abbot had a tendency to ask rhetorical questions, as in a sermon: it might be best not to interrupt. A hare darted out from the alders, stopped, twitched its nose, and loped back the way it had come. Even that made them want to laugh. Brother Gideon knew exactly what to do, of course: in fact, he was miffed that he hadn't already been asked for advice, until he remembered that Father Jeremy regarded your previous life and its possible expertise as not just there to be pillaged. There were limits. He quelled the egotistical moment (the demolition business had raised him in the eyes of his brothers, and this had unduly pleased him) and took a deep breath instead, sucking God's eternal breath out of the fenland air and into his soul.

The giant angel with the freckly nose. It all made sense.

He closed his eyes. It was good to say it. He had to. He was full of God's breath.

'Helicopter.'

'Sorry, Brother Gideon?'

'You could hire a helicopter.' The brothers chuckled. 'Sounds crazy, but it's what you do in these circs. Not the kind of rescue helicopter that lands on motorways after a car crash or winches people off burning decks, but the freight type. That carries trucks or girders or trees beneath it. They're called Skycranes. Sikorsky, but owned by Erickson. Very powerful. Six-blade fan on top. Two massive Pratt & Whitney turboshafts producing about four thousand horsepower, so they can lift a large bus no probs. Our cross is a feather, in comparison.'

He stopped. He was back in his cream suit, his Zanotti white leather high-tops, his splash of Serge Lutens's Fumerie Turque. It was instant and horrible. At the same time, he had been granted a vision. A true vision! He was being torn in two, between new spirit and old flesh. No, they were meeting in his head with a big surge of complicated currents, a crash of foam. He wiped his face and felt giddy.

The brothers were gawping at him, glints of eyes inside their deep, warm hoods.

Father Jeremy urged him to continue. He did so.

'If we loosen the cement base with lots of water hosed in around, and wrap the entire construction in a safety tarp, the cross can be plucked out and hauled aloft and deposited somewhere suitable near the smithy. And the same operation for the return journey. We can redo the base properly . . .'

He heard the cold sludge of cement tumbling in its mixer, the high ring of scaffolding going up, the fumy rumbles of London like a pang – all the old excitements. He had felt the same during the extension's demolition, but with less pleasure. 'I know helicopter hire firms I used to work with. Special rate. I gave them so much business . . .'

A sudden commotion. He found himself on his knees in the attractive little ferns. The brothers were looking down at him, concerned. 'Pulled out like a tooth,' he mumbled, hands on his head. Then he apologised and got to his feet without help, although it was offered, pushing his glasses back up his nose.

'How very interesting,' Father Jeremy commented. Brother

Gideon assumed this was referring to the helicopter idea, not the wobbly moment.

Returned to his cell, he put a line through his marginal *worthless imaginings* note. And added a large: 'Sorry, Lord!'

*

But the fact is, once the surge had departed, he felt positively beatific. He couldn't say why to the others: it was too showy, even embarrassing. The monks here denied the ego as much as they could. The general consensus was that you slowly disappeared into the majesty of God; Brother Gideon imagined it as a kind of translucent golden robe made up of endless tissuey folds in which they were scattered like tiny crumbs. Or, as Thomas Merton put it: 'We surrender our lives into the hands of God and never take them back.' Never!

Vast, elderly but strong hands. Your father's hands when you were small. Why not your mother's hands? Because we are tied to conventional notions. God only knows what God's hands really look like. Not like a GP's, he hoped. Waxy white and soap-smelling. A vet's, maybe. Able to handle everything from bulls to kittens.

It was not a conventional vision, either: the Virgin had not appeared on the cloister lawn or in the vegetable garden, as had happened to more than one brother – her sandals glittering between the cabbages, her slender finger raised. No, he had simply been granted a vision, in the form of a precognitive dream: the helicopter as an angel. Rotors for wings! And, of course, it was faintly ridiculous to anyone but him. What he should have done is recounted his dream beforehand; now it felt a bit lame.

Yes, it was clearly a sign that said GOD AT WORK, as clear as a weave of Red Arrows, smoke trails in a blue sky. It proved His presence, an engagement even in such trivial matters as a minor Trappist monastery's repairs, but to anyone else it would sound, at this stage, like a silly anecdote. 'Oh, *that's* funny, I dreamed about the

Twin Towers collapsing a year or two back, except they didn't look like the Twin Towers, they looked like a couple of cucumbers.' It was on that level, for anyone else but the vision's recipient.

Anyway, what would he gain by boasting about his dream? It was a private message, just something between him and the Creator. A little leg-up, wiping him free of the blur of doubt. Another few cylinders on his zeal.

He allowed himself to drift again into the seamless ocean of chants and prayers in the duskiness of the church, every brother's face somehow nobler in the soft candlelight of lauds or vespers. He struggled not to feel a head higher. Plump with his store of secret knowledge. Once, during the blissful, smoky murk of compline, he scratched his rugby-squashed nose, squeezing his eyes shut as if wringing out a lemon.

Ad te clamamus exsules filii Hevæ,
Ad te suspiramus, gementes et flentes . . .

His eyes popped open again. Our Lady's face in painted wood, full of compassion in the single candle's glare. The angel's face was real, like flesh. Why would an angel be so endearingly toothy? Did they not have orthodontists in heaven? He was chanting without listening; his mind adrift. The silence began after the last prayer and would hold firm until lauds in seven hours' time. Silence and stillness that, as they all fanned out from the sweet-fumed cavern of a church to their separate cells on a whisper of leather soles, were moving towards him with the open arms of complete freedom.

The others noticed the change in him and commented on it during the weekly walks. Had he seemed that miserable and beaten down before? They told him he had a spring in his step, a brilliance in his eyes. His bursts of jolly whistling as he gardened amused them, although Father Jeremy said that it might be wise to 'keep the volume down' as some of the boppier tunes were going 'round and round' his head. WE LIVE IN SILENCE. It was the abbot's way of saying 'Shut Up'.

'It's the chopper!' they all agreed, benignly teasing him. They were skirting a muddy patch near a creek, stepping between bluebells and the tiny croziers of juvenile bracken. But they also agreed that it was 'a brilliant idea'. Now would have been the moment to have told them who had given him the idea, but he stalled. It had all been arranged: the firm was lifting thirty tons of extractor fans onto a shopping centre in Grantham in a few days – just up the road for a helicopter. The cross would be another unit, that's all. Brother Gideon had checked out the cement base, lifting up his habit and kneeling: it was surprisingly unstable, fissured by frosts and age. Amazing, really, that the cross was still upright: he guessed the damage went deep. It would be like tugging out a fence post, once they'd pumped a bit of water into the surrounding soil.

'I can't deny I'm fairly excited,' he admitted, endearing himself further to the team. For the first time he felt part of a combine, on a purely superficial level. He belonged. It had taken four years. And on a deeper level, he belonged to God. To Christ. To Christ's abiding love. It was all still a mystery, but no longer a fantastical one. He had found his true vocation, the answer to his essential chronic dissatisfaction. This had built up and up until he had exploded mentally and sinned in a disgusting manner, hurting someone else, but it had lanced the boil. He had not lost all hope of being taken into the majesty of the Lord, that translucent golden robe in which he was a crumb, because divine forgiveness was Christianity's steel truss. Quite unique.

Now he knew that the angel in his dream was a genuine visitation. A mediator. Beamed into his mind, or whatever. Effortlessly carrying the burden. Still he kept it to himself: individual modesty was the mainstay of the community. He would not spiritually lord it over the others. He would not even consider whether he was impressing them. It was irrelevant.

Best not to conjecture on the actual workings of the visitation. It was like thinking of the six million – or was it six billion? – galaxies in the known universe and trying to comprehend what that number meant, what it *actually* meant, the whole thing. A beam of sunlight fell through the kitchen window above the huge sink and flashed on the copper skillet that he was in the middle of scrubbing. He was here, he was alive. The huge and vaulted kitchens smelled of damp sponges and Ajax and interminable simmerings of lentil soup. His keel had struck the shore of another day and here he was, right in this moment. No task was ever so hurried that you couldn't stop and marvel.

*

Brother Odilo took more photographs and emailed them to Jim in the half-hour window when Wi-Fi was permitted. Then Jim came himself and took more photos and a video, as well as measurements. Brother Gideon left Brother Odilo to handle this side of the job, merely glimpsing the activity from the fudge-making room, which happened to offer a good view of the cross: he saw that Jim was a broad-shouldered man with a bushy, somewhat hippyish brown beard; he stood at the top of a ladder set against the firm crosspiece. The humble workman without whom the world would not function, yet who goes entirely unrecognised. Brother Gideon's quiet pleasure in this sight broadened in turn to include the entire monastery and its fenland surrounds in a beneficent, shimmering globe of generosity and compassion.

He had barely left this place in four years and each time it had been like walking into the middle of a football crowd just as a late goal was scored. He had forgotten how the modern world was. Noise and stridency and speed. And he'd mostly gone no further, on a monastery bicycle, than the local village, which to most people was as quiet as the grave (albeit a pretty one). His one trip to Lincoln on a grey January day last year (to have a benign carcinoma on his chin removed, combining the outing with a cathedral concert) was overwhelming: a second Mumbai, one giant yell. He'd had to retreat to a quiet public park after his appointment, meditating on the miracle of Creation. Swans! By the time the concert was over, and he'd descended onto the high street to find a taxi (the last bus long gone), the city centre was transfigured into hell, the two cathedral towers helpless to intervene: it was worse than London had ever been. Paralytic hordes slipping on vomit, demonic yells and screams, men walking about with broken cocktail glasses in their pockets to thrust into the faces of passers-by (according to Brother Simeon, anyway, who knew these things). A crowd of scantily clad girls appeared around the corner and he was goosed. Squeals of mad laughter. A monk's robes were no protection whatsoever. They'd thought he was a yoof dressed up for a club special.

When his father had suddenly dropped dead before Christmas, the family had to be content with prayers: Skye was much too far, and he hadn't seen the bristly drunk of an old buffer for ten years. Father Jeremy acquiesced: 'I'm sorry you couldn't have healed the breach. I would not have hesitated to let you go. But sometimes the healing has to await the life after. Complicated! Your new family here will all pray for your dear dad's soul, of course.'

Yes, he'd never been so content as in this place, or at least not since his childhood. Despite Dad's whisky-laced tantrums, his childhood was happy up to his parents' divorce and the sudden brutality and loneliness of boarding school in Yorkshire. Where Dad had been as happy as a lamb – or rather, as an alpha wolf.

And then, three days later, right in the middle of compline, he felt his father's presence and it was shimmering with love, as if gilded. He covered his face with his hands and wept silently. No one knew why, no one wanted to know why.

WE LIVE IN SILENCE.

Soon after Jim's recce, Brother Odilo went off to the smithy to discuss the job. He tucked his scapular into his cord belt and zoomed away (well, bumped over the sloshy ruts) in the monastery's mud-splattered Mitsubishi jeep. He returned a few hours later with an iron weathervane in the shape of a monk, lots of unmerciful words about HGVs 'hogging the lanes at a top speed of forty', and some surprising news.

He shared it at an extraordinary meeting held in the chapter house, the candles augmented by new and rather natty LEDs suspended from the vault on wires. Tasteful, it had to be said: Brother Gideon was always consulted, these days, over any changes to the abbey's fabric or interior accoutrements.

The blacksmith wouldn't hear of it, they were told.

A collective steam valve opened, or so it sounded like. Father Jeremy pulled a long face.

'Of a helicopter being used, that is,' said Brother Odilo. Jim was ecologically minded and felt that a helicopter, apart from burning far too much fuel, was not right for the simple life of a monastery.

'Always struck me as being a bit short of celebrity game show,' said Brother Simeon. 'Remember *The Interceptor?*'

'Is Jim altogether there?' asked Brother William, probably rhetorically.

'Perfectly sane,' Brother Odilo smiled. Jim had studied the matter carefully and had decided it would be quite possible to work on the cross in its vertical position, with the help of a harness, the type that tree surgeons use.

'What about the toing and froing?' asked Father Jeremy.

'He suggests he and his son stay in the guest house for a week and that they use our own smithy, modest though it is.'

'It hasn't been operative for years.'

'It has an anvil and a forge. We'll supply the fuel. No travel costs, as it were.' Brother Odilo's round specs flashed. 'And he'll charge the minimum for his labour.'

'Oh, jolly good,' said Brother Saul, who was in charge of finances. They all grinned (except for one).

'He has always been interested in monasteries, in the simple life,' Brother Odilo went on. 'He said something rather beautiful: you spend money, but you don't spend memories.'

'Does he feel the call?'

'I'm not sure about that, Father. He rather keeps the local pub going, and not just because he put in a couple of iron braces.'

They all (almost all) laughed softly, like dons. The shadows in the chapter house seemed to recoil in shock, nevertheless. Brother Gideon's glasses were misting up.

'Merton liked a tipple,' said Brother Perry from New Zealand, who was even gaunter than the others – including Brother Gideon.

'And was not averse to skirt,' added Brother Simeon, who often went a bit too far.

'I think,' Brother Odilo continued hastily, 'Jim was hoping he might be shown around. I mean, the parts the tourists don't reach.'

'Oh, perfectly possible, though we're not very exciting, are we?'

'As long as he doesn't want to look at *all* our parts,' joked Brother Simeon, who now and again went much too far.

The others chuckled dutifully, except for Brother Felix, hard of hearing and fiddling with his hearing aids. (And one other among them, of course.)

'Poor Brother Gideon,' said a voice. 'No celebrity chopper after all.'

It was Brother Simeon again, directly under an LED spot so that his thinning, sandy hair gleamed like an aureole.

The target of his ironic compassion was feeling an obscure sense of betrayal and, in his physical body, sharp cramps. 'Oh, it doesn't matter,' he said, blinking, emerging as if from a meditative trance. 'Next time!'

'On a happier note,' said Father Jeremy, raising his index finger as if indicating the source of the bounty, 'East Midlands branches are stocking our brandy fudge in all their Lincolnshire branches as part of their regional sourcing programme. This is good news, as there is fierce competition from Polish fudge, these days.'

'Polish fudge is apparently delicious,' wheezed Brother William, in charge of fudge-making. 'And competitively priced, of course.'

Father Jeremy nodded politely. 'They – East Midlands – have issues with the walnut fudge on health and safety grounds. They are seriously considering our biscotti. They would, however, like to relabel Our Lady of Grace Fudge. They propose Monk's Lincolnshire Fudge. I see no objection, if the new nomenclature remains exclusive to them. Any comments?'

'Yummy gummy,' said Brother Simeon.

He had eagerly entered into the treasure house within him, he had seen the things that are in heaven, as St Isaac the Syrian had once put it, and now there was a dark screen yanked in front. Again he dreamed of the cross, suddenly sprouting bats' wings and lumbering into the air only to crash into the sea, himself cheering. In another dream he was looking at the real Jesus on the Cross, only his nails were clothes pegs. 'I got wet,' said the Saviour, in a drippy voice, 'and they've hung me up to dry.' Was that God's idea of a joke? He did recall his mother hanging his teddy bear up to dry on the clothes line, when he was seven or eight: pegged by the paws. Poor Teddybuns. Poor Jesus.

He requested a meeting – not a confessional – with Father Jeremy. He felt that he was being tested. Then he cancelled. The 'chopper' business had become a harmless joke. If he told Father Jeremy the truth, he would never be taken seriously again. And anyway, what could the abbot do?

'The Lord moves in mysterious ways,' he'd be bound to say. 'Which is all the more reason we should be fully awake to them. It is all a great adventure.'

Yes, like canoeing up the Orinoco. Which the abbot had once done, apparently, in his former life.

In the solitude of his cell, in his sacred desert, Brother Gideon prayed so hard that his knuckles showed teeth marks. He had to adopt a mask of jollity when necessary, to avoid the others thinking he had fallen into depression just because a whirlybird was no longer needed. Keeping so awake to God's mystery meant he would nod off during the psalms of none, finding the usual nap at midday impossible. It was not just the noonday Devil, stalking the grace and energy of a monk's calling with the leaden tread of sloth and inattention, it was the sense of some transcendent curve having been casually broken. 'Let nothing be put before the work of God': Rule of St Benedict, chapter 3. Right to the end he believed that some divine force would intervene, clattering its blades.

So he felt bewildered when he eventually heard the sharp hammer-strokes through the arched gate, their echo caught in the cloisters and hurled about like a metal ball. They were like a parody of the bells, which had a tendency to thump behind their tunefulness. The blacksmith's son, called Larry, was a muscular lad with fine girlish features; he would remove his shirt, showing skin tanned by the great outdoors, glazed like the monks' earthenware platters – but, in his case, with sweat. He had a smell about him that was faintly sweet: passing him now and again, Brother Gideon felt troubled by an attraction that was completely involuntary and ridiculous, as if planted by an outside force, and which suffused his chalky pallor with a blush. Had he suddenly turned gay? Had he always been gay underneath?

Occasionally he suffered torments of concupiscent desire, but this always involved voluptuous females that, if he'd ever believed in old-style devils, were almost too obviously the latter's corny, vulgar creations straight from the netherworld of porn. Chastity was supposed to be the hardest vow of all, but it had never been too much of a struggle to sublimate hot lust with a cold douche of prayer and exercise, or even to lose it in the densely branching threnodies of Gregorian chant. Hair shirts were a thing of the past. Like many of the brothers, he had a face out of El Greco, bony and taut-skinned, but that's as far as it went. That sort of darkly ecstatic, over-egged Catholicism, dripping with Christ's blood and pungent with guilt, was as alien to him as Islam.

When, in his novitiate period, he had asked Father Jeremy about Christ's awkward deviation in Matthew 13 from the theme of forgiveness and love, the abbot had started by fobbing him off again with the Hell-is-isolation-from-God line – a hell whose pain we cannot conceive of, nevertheless.

'So Buddhists are doomed to burn, Father. No omniscient creator. No God.'

Father Jeremy nodded benignly, although his broad forehead was creased with concentration. 'I am not a specialist in Buddhism, I'm afraid, although I have always understood that its various forms are not aspects of faith, but of a way of being. Am I right?'

Brother Gideon sighed and turned his eyes to the ceiling, very much the anxious novice. The abbot picked up his pen and tapped the table with it, deliberately rather than carelessly. 'Do you know what that sound is?'

'Impatience with silly questions.'

Father Jeremy gave a brief chortle. 'No, not at all. It is the clink of what John Ruskin called the "dreadful hammers" of the geologists that he heard at the end of every biblical verse. We have far more to challenge us than other belief systems.'

'Black holes? Dinosaurs?'

Father Jeremy nodded. 'The real mystery, as I see it, is why God created a world full of fifty-foot predators with crocodile brains and jaws armed with bone-crunching teeth. They hunted in packs, you know. Or should we say flocks, as with modern birds. It went on for 150 million years, to no apparent purpose.'

'The Almighty is very patient.'

'Precisely. And so completely mysterious.'

Brother Gideon gave up after a few of these rather cerebral outings; truth was not going to be obtained through discussion, but by living in a space that allowed you the freedom to reflect and pray and simply be alive in the Eternal Presence. The traditional certainties had all been demolished, officially. Sometimes his entire faith felt like a counselling session, with a few characters in funny costumes invited in to role-play. Yet he would still taste a sudden, transcorporeal sweetness that almost had him swooning, and at the most unlikely moments. The rest – the monastic existence overall – was at the very least a kind of mutual reinforcement.

For all his spiritual ramparts, the hammering and a metal-cutting saw's awful whine began to make inroads on the recesses of his heart. He appreciated much more keenly the hours of prayer and meditation before dawn, in the darkness, before the world bustled into busyness.

His conclusions were not comforting.

The helicopter had been nothing else but God's will, announced to him beforehand in a vision. Jim was a massive hulk who drank. He had a ponytail, a relic of his youth, but it made him look like a genuine barbarian. A Vandal or a Visigoth. His smell was peppery, his T-shirt (inscribed HEAVY METAL ARTIST in Gothic lettering) revealed a thicket of hair at the armpits. He would don his leather apron and yell jovially at his son, whose naked shoulders and chest were so smooth, so anatomical, they looked sculpted. Perhaps father and son were from evil's shadowy realm, and not humble manual labourers after all. Cunning infiltrators who would despoil the sacred tree. Who, after all, had forged the nails of torment for Golgotha? Evil sometimes cohered into the concrete. You could smell it.

If he happened to walk past either of these so-called guests, he would retreat into the shadows of his hood or, if the hood was down, lower his head and watch a pair of sandalled feet slip in and out of his habit's hem as if they had nothing to do with him. The need for silence, of course, made it easier: but the lack of even a nod must have puzzled them. And secretly, his hands hidden in his voluminous white sleeves, Brother Gideon would make the sign of the cross.

On Saturday morning the following week, exactly on schedule, Jim unbuckled his safety harness and folded the vertiginous ladder for the last time. Apart from the struts, ties and braces, he had protected the skyward edges of the cross with a thin sheeting of lead. On Sunday, after none, instead of trotting off on their walk, the brothers gathered around the cross and applauded – Brother Gideon joining in with fake enthusiasm. Despite his prayers, a part of him still felt that he'd been taken for a ride. Perhaps the Almighty had a sense of humour! The air was warm in the sun: it was almost June. The local press was present, in the form of a gingery youth with an exaggerated telephoto lens, its shutter sounding far too often.

'I'll let you in on a secret,' announced Jim. Like his son, he had put on his best shirt and jacket, washed and combed his hair, so that he looked like someone else. 'You know them roof bosses in the cathedrals? So high up you can't even see the carvings? That's because they did 'em for God, not people. Well, I'm a woodworker as well as a smith and I've – sorry, Larry, *we* have – done the same. Right on the top. A little secret summat. Just in case,' he added slyly, with a laugh – for he knew the brothers were aware that he was not a firm believer.

Father Jeremy gave a little speech, but Brother Gideon wasn't listening.

He thought he knew what Jim had carved into the top of the cross. This secret thing. What a relief this was.

As agreed, they showed the blacksmith and his son around the monastery. Jim and Larry shuffled beside the brothers with the awkwardness of novitiates. Larry asked if it was true that they had neither radio, television nor any means of listening to music, and limited Wi-Fi for only half an hour (strictly supervised by Father Jeremy). 'Well, I'm the cat's mother,' he said, softly. The cells were tidy, sparse and spotless, not in any way interesting. The visit only took a couple of hours, including the chapel with its remnants of pre-dissolution days, a few stones and columnar bases out of all that havoc.

There were several rooms that had not been opened for years, their cobwebbed shutters creaking wide, light pouring in, dust swirling and glittering over pockmarked benches and bare flooring, a mustiness of neglect. At one time there had been fifty monks, now there were fifteen. Jim wondered about the attics, so up they went. A lot of junk and mice droppings and discarded balls of birds' nests. Beams from the fifteenth century, with carpenters' marks like cuts in bread. This part of the tour, at least, was an adventure.

Except that Brother Simeon kept making jokes. St Benedict said this was wrong, of course. Not to speak words that are vain or such as provoke laughter. Not to love noisy laughter. Brother Simeon practically cackled, and Prior Christian from the mean streets of Middlesbrough joined in.

Brother Simeon: 'Looks like we're too late. The Fifth Horseman of the Apocalypse has already been through.'

Prior Christian: 'Not before dropping off at my old local in sunny Middlesbrough. Know what it was called, Jim?'

'Er, let me think. The Black Horse?'

'Last Orders.'

Uproar. Nothing was said.

They had a small celebration on the cloister lawn, less sharply mown these days for ecological reasons and thickly sprinkled with daisies and buttercups, soft with clover, popular with butterflies.

Brother Gideon had already sneaked away. He just needed something verified. He slipped out of the main gate. No one had seen him go, he felt certain of it. WE LIVE IN SILENCE.

The extendable ladder was a sturdy model: it was surprisingly heavy and awkward to unfold. It creaked under his sandalled feet as he fought his vertigo, his black scapular thrown over his shoulder as it always was when he gardened, beat the fudge mix, worked the cross-cut handsaw through the logs, whatever. Up and up, step by step, dogged and quivering, don't look down, don't think about looking down, don't think about anything but going up, rung by metallic rung. Gripping the ladder's stiles, steady does it. All in the mind.

The tips of Christ's flimsy loincloth, depicted by the sculptor as rippling away in a strong wind, jutted out beyond the edge of the vertical beam. He was only just past them and it already felt amazingly high, much higher than it looked from down below: he was about two-thirds of the way up. His heart thumped in his throat. He felt vertigo pulling on his cowl, trying to unbalance him as he clasped the stiles, eyes now screwed tightly shut. This was what it had been like, once, on scaffolding, talking to builders and so on, but there was always a safety rail, often a tarp tied on, bright hard hats, sensible boots. Not sandals, about as useless as flip-flops! Had he set the ladder correctly against the wood? At the right angle? He knew from his former life that the angle was important. Seventy degrees. The ladder seemed to wobble slightly: was the crosspiece slippery in some way?

Angles. Angels. Not angles, but angels! He chuckled to himself, even more certain of what he would find on the summit.

Up one rung at a time. Mind over mind. Vertigo was all in the mind. Lord, bring me to fulfilment . . . It helped when he reached the cross-beam, its close detail of iron-like timber. Don't look out at the horizon, the fuzz of treetops on the fens, the shimmer of the salt marshes and beyond them the haze of the North Sea. He wouldn't mind being out there right now, lying in the dune grass.

The blacksmith was a head taller than him. The ladder's last three rungs were above the cross-beam, and therefore unscalable, but the beam's thick wood stopped the next rung down from being used as a full support. He was still too low to examine the very top of the cross. This would be his only chance. His long, voluminous gear was completely unsuitable for this exercise, and the rungs were biting into his thin soles. Vertigo began to invade him again: he could hardly breathe, his heart pounding in imminent panic. He closed his eyes and sent a little bubble of prayer up through the depths towards the safe, sunlit surface.

The apex of the cross was inches away. He put one foot into the next rung as far as it could go – no deeper than the knuckles of his toes – and pressed down on the metal strip to raise himself up, the other foot dangling for a moment as he released the stile on the inner side and used that free arm to embrace the cross's vertical as best he could. Thus, leaning sideways and up, his sight line began to clear the summit. All his weight, his life, depended on the grip of his toes in their slippery footwear. It was a test. He was being tested. Technically, in terms of health and safety, he was doing everything wrong. He had no wings to break a fall, to glide away from the hideous impact of the ground, the stiles weren't tied and he was leaning out. But he mustn't think of the ground, incredibly far below.

He edged his head up over the square pinnacle of the cross. The rectangular space, like a tiny stage, newly coated with protective oil, had fissures in it. Carved fissures. Gullies and chasms. Hard to interpret, but surely a cuneiform of feathers, pinions, feet, a broad and toothy smile . . . He reached up higher, stretching his neck, his taut leg taking most of his weight, the toes in their agonised monkey grip (though he wasn't a monkey, had fallen out of practice for these past millions of years), the calf muscles beginning to quiver, to tremble, even to spasm.

The gullies and chasms played an optical trick on him, suddenly. From this higher angle, they congealed into something else. The scrolled initials J and L. A dainty hammer and tongs side by side. A date that was last week. Nothing more on the weather-worn wood. No angel, with chiselled wings outspread. Nothing remotely angelic.

Now, utterly crestfallen, he almost expected to see something obscene scratched on: a cartoon pair of breasts. A swollen dick or two. Bodies grappling. A bird had already struck: an exploding nebula of greenish white. Probably a crow.

It was all his fault. He had second-guessed God. He had adhered, not to God, but to his own self, his own selfish desires and surface expectations. Instead of gold in the flame of God, he was flesh, charred beyond recognition. The leg that was barely his own gave a violent spasm, his arm slipped from the bulky beam, the construction of his entire body began to disintegrate, made no sense, his toes relinquishing their hopeless station as he found no resistance in the air's implacable neutrality, passing through it effortlessly with his legs pedalling in slow motion and his arms waving in vast circles as if tracing the spin of galaxies.

The land had flattened out to one concussion. Hurt. Up there was the sky's curve, interrupted by shadows of heads, puppet shapes, in and out. Voices dim over the ringing. Something soft under his chin. A wiping at his mouth, which he didn't like, it was inside his chest that he needed succour. Or maybe his chest was inside his head, beating and fiery.

He was a laughing stock. The heavens were guffawing. Where was this noise? Was it outside him? It was the noise that was beating and fiery. Right up above him, in the quivering wheel of sky, there was something with a long curving tail like a mayfly's. A golden-yellow mayfly, very bright in its yellowness.

You've come to uproot the painful tooth, its agonising nails.

Thump thump thump. Incredibly loud.

The chopper began its descent into the field, making the trees shake, sending up dust, grit and dry sheep droppings. The brothers were bent double with merriment, bending into the great rush of wind, holding their unruly habits down with their hands. He was still dreaming, perhaps. He saw it all very clearly. The bells of lauds would sound at any moment, thumping him awake.

He saw the golden machine settle, its thin rotor blades slow with a whine. Of course. Men in bright orange jackets running towards him down the side of his vision, immensely tall.

Someone's burning hand tightening on his. Another on his brow, scorching. A pale face looming through the blur.

He opened his mouth to say, 'O my angel, my angel, my pure and lovely angel!'

But nothing came out of the sudden silence, unless that dim yelp had been his, after all. ■

Will Alexander

Enjaracon Sponaeda

a hyper-dimensional reality 'bending or changing space-time'
W.A.

'I have crossed this sub-conjoined vacuum
with its ominous tenet
with its emptiness of hydroxyl
across untraceable radiation
not of the dissonance of a visible body   sans physiology constricted
   as barrier sans irradiated happenstance

the Milky Way has summoned me
in the midst of its 10th volution
of its 10th centrifugation
to an obscure spur
¾'s out from its mean

maybe I could be classified
as trans-solar in nature
as inter-cosmic residue
as circum-planetary crystal
housed in spurting sapphire amphorae thus
I loom in human vicinity
not unlike a noiseless solar oak listening to chaos transpiring

certainly I am not here due to trans-saurian manipulation
or to the toneless kindlings of the Greys
insisting as they do on capturable form
on dry explosives
on incalculable nerve length

what I say remains absent of the contiguous
as if I shifted between the sound of otters or the silence of snail grass
  shifting through land rays

sidling through inclement neon
it can be asked from certain quarters how can I possibly be?

how can all the pressures of surveillance
fail to describe me?

how can it fail to know I have vanished & returned to myself over
  countless conundrums
over resurrections 12 billion years in the making?

never knowing that my body is a structureless compendium?

at my spawning terra luna was unknown
its life as orb had never spun
all of this I've known within a flash of supranoesis

which tests the topography of corpses the relativity of geography &
  its entropy
with its capillaries
with its challenged fertilities

here I am casting glow sans measurable scale & its fractions without
  hissing
without coded political inscription casting less weight than
  mesmeric Saturns
less weight than stained red suns emerging from shards of
  incipience spawned from other realms & dimensions

which
unlike the form of terra luna
has no force of armies
no flank of human armies roaming inside their moons

thus
I have no interest concerning ozone starvation on Phobos
or couriers of serpents roaming the plains of Mars

knowing as I know the bleach of scorched neutrinos
the intangible waves of scorched secondary powers
of in-cautionary fumes
as if I had mined simple forms of microbes
as would a shamanistic mongoose suspended above a particle of
  floods . . .'

AUTHOR'S NOTE: Enjaracon Sponaeda is the name of the humanoid alien speaking.

Sarah Gerard with her parents, Pat and Eric, outside H. Stern Jewelers at the Fontainebleau Hotel, Miami Beach, 1991
Courtesy of the author

GOING DIAMOND

Sarah Gerard

I was seven when my parents joined Amway. Our house filled up with Amway products: boxes of Nutrilite™ vitamins, toaster pastries, Glister™ toothpaste, Artistry™ makeup. We washed our hair with Satinique shampoo; we washed our floors with L.O.C.™ cleaner; we washed our dishes with Amway-brand dish soap. Our friends were Amway. Our vocabulary was Amway. We were 'Directs' going 'Diamond'. We 'showed The Plan' to anyone who listened.

We drove to Miami for 'functions' at the Fontainebleau Hotel. Thousands of people attended, all packed into the big ballroom with lights turned up and people dancing in the aisles, getting 'fired up' to Calloway's 'I Wanna Be Rich', which blasted over the speakers. We clapped our hands and sang along.

A man took the stage with a microphone – a *Diamond!* – followed by a woman in a ballgown – another Diamond! Another Diamond and another and another, all shining under spotlights, smiling – their success itself a luminous aura engulfing them. 'DO YOU WANT YOUR DREAM TO BECOME A REALITY?' the man yelled, strutting and flashing his teeth. 'WHO'S GOT A DREAM?'

We had a dream!

'I SAID WHO'S GOT A DREAM?'

We did!

Amway is a multilevel marketing corporation. Some call it a pyramid scheme. In 2015, its parent company, Alticor, claimed transglobal sales of $9.5 billion. Amway is the biggest direct-selling company in the world. Distributors make money by signing up other distributors and – somewhere in the background – 'selling' Amway products. It's not exactly clear how Amway products should reach the public. That isn't part of Amway's marketing plan; the plan mostly teaches distributors how to sign up other distributors, to whom they then distribute Amway products, who then distribute Amway products to other distributors they sign up, and onward. It's been the subject, along with its affiliate companies, of multimillion-dollar lawsuits and other legal actions on almost every continent.

If it's not your family who brings you in, it's probably a friend. For my dad, it was a manager at one of the car dealerships for which he handled advertising. The man's business comprised almost half of my dad's income. Over time, they'd developed a friendship. You'd think my dad would have been immune to Amway, given his familiarity with advertising's insidious ways. But how does the saying go? A good salesman can sell you your own grandmother.

My parents and I were solidly middle class when we collided with Amway. We owned our home. We lived in a safe neighborhood where I could play outside without supervision and walk home alone after the sun went down. We always kept an excess of food in the house. I got new shoes whenever I outgrew my old pair. I received new toys when my old ones broke and new books when I finished reading the ones I had. I went to gymnastics practice four times a week, singing lessons once a week, camp over the summer, and back-to-school shopping in the fall. We didn't need Amway.

But that didn't matter. In Amway, there's no such thing as contentment.

If you're happy with what you have, you haven't dreamed, says Amway. Your life could be faster, shinier, brighter, more spacious – don't settle for less. Join Amway.

A mway cofounders Rich DeVos and Jay Van Andel commissioned Wilbur Cross to write the first 'official' history of the Amway Corporation. In the book, Cross repeatedly references the work of Shad Helmstetter, PhD, a 'motivational expert' specializing in 'programming' yourself to change negative self-talk into positive self-talk. Negativity is expressly verboten in the world of Amway, as it breeds doubt – distributors are advised to get rid of any negative people in their downline as soon as possible if they can't train them to be positive.

There are long sections in *Amway* dedicated to teaching readers how to go about programming others to be positive – you are helping people in this way: 'You can offer them hope when they feel as though they are in a hopeless situation.' In fact, Cross says, it may be in your best interest to seek out the most hopeless and lonely people you know and invite them to become Amway distributors – sometimes 'negative people turn out to be the best prospects of all' because they are the ones who really need Amway most – 'they are the ones who are looking for something else in life'.

Dreambuilding is more than wishful thinking, Cross explains. It's more than seeing what people with more money have and wishing you had it. Dreambuilding is 'the perfection of excellence'; 'It is a way to control what you *think*, to enhance what you *believe*, and to solidify your *attitude*.' Most importantly, it's a procedure, 'a skill that has to be learned, practiced, and put into action'.

W e slipped Amway motivational tapes into our car's tape deck, and listened, and repeated. We bought tickets to Amway functions for $50 a pop and booked hotel rooms nearby to attend them. We sampled the products and demonstrated our commitment by filling our house with box upon box of Amway goods. We made lists. We framed pictures. We drew diagrams. We hosted seminars in our home where we lectured our downline to 'activate their dreams'. We constantly reminded ourselves that our dreams were possible. We only interacted with others who affirmed this. We took photographs of each other inside our dreams: Here I am, a skinny nine-year-old posing proudly next to a kidney-shaped pool. Here's my mother in a pair of khaki shorts and a Hawaiian shirt descending a marble staircase. And my father, two thumbs up, lying on a king-sized canopy bed. We visualized, yes – but then we went one step further and *made visual*. We stepped inside our dreams, literally.

The country was in the last gasps of the Great Depression. Rich DeVos was fourteen. He was walking two miles through the snow to his high school each day, in his hometown of Grand Rapids, Michigan: wool collar popped high, galoshes squishing, wind in his face. Occasionally he would take the streetcar or city bus – but allowing time for the city bus meant having to rise long before the sun came up. 'I needed more efficient transportation, and already being an enterprising type, I had an idea,' he writes.

Enter Jay Van Andel, Amway's other cofounder. Jay had a 1929 Ford Model A, which Rich had noticed both driving down his street and also parked outside his high school. 'I thought a ride in this car would surely beat the bus, a streetcar, or walking,' says Rich. The rest is as saccharine as you would expect: good American boys working hard to make their dreams come true.

Rich and Jay go into business together selling Nutrilite™ vitamins, an early multilevel marketing scheme for which Jay's second cousin and his parents are already distributors. When Nutrilite™ goes kaput in 1948 after an FDA crackdown on their 'excessive claims' regarding the products' nutritional values, Rich and Jay strike out on their own – the American Way.

At the heart of Amway is the love of 'free enterprise' – an equal-opportunity system in which determination alone is the path to achievement. If you have a dream, Amway says, and you try hard enough to achieve that dream, and let nothing stand in your way, then success is guaranteed. That is the promise of what Rich DeVos calls 'Compassionate Capitalism' – helping people help themselves.

Rich and Jay set up shop in Rich's basement selling Liquid Organic Cleaner™, or L.O.C.™, Amway's first original product. With their trust in each other and the support of their loving wives they're able to weather all bumps on their ride to the top, including the first federal investigation of Amway, by the Federal Trade Commission in 1975. In a chapter entitled 'The Critics Weigh In' (in part two of Cross's book, called 'Selling America'), Rich says of the suit, 'we considered the suit another government misunderstanding of business principles and an attack on free enterprise.' Anything that challenges Amway – particularly the government – challenges free enterprise, and thus freedom itself. If you need proof of Amway's principles, just look at all the people who've benefited from Amway, Rich tells us: millions worldwide.

I loved the days when we'd go Dreambuilding at the Bayou Club as a family. We began going immediately after joining Amway, when I was in second grade. The development was new, still under construction. There was space between the houses and the far stretch of the golf course undulating luxuriously around them. Model homes rose from the landscape like castles, bigger than any houses I'd ever seen – and vacant. Never occupied. Empty dreams, waiting to be filled.

As a child, the pleasure of being inside a big house was endless. Future ownership had come to feel like a guarantee, so I took to imagining what life would be like in each one we visited. In this model of a girl's bedroom with its shelf of figurines, canopy bed with lace cover, pink-painted chest, and carved mirror, contentment felt within reach. This room was assurance I'd never be lonely or bored; that I would always have something lovely to look at and lovely things to say and other children near me to validate my worth. I felt special, included.

Imagine watching movies in this home theater. Imagine riding an elevator up to my dream bedroom. Imagine swimming in this pool each afternoon. Eating meals in this dining room under an opulent chandelier. Sometimes we brought along a camera and took pictures of each other walking around the houses. We saw two or three in a day and then took the film to be developed. Back in our three-bedroom, we looked at the photos together, then stored them in fresh albums. In the photos, we wore the same outfits while the houses around us changed.

We were the proud owners of three beautiful homes, the photos said.

Limitation on ownership was not a concept I was familiar with as a middle-class child – everything could be mine. 'Spoiled' was a word I heard often from family and friends, and I was proud of it. I thought I deserved to be spoiled – I was fully ignorant of the negative connotations of the word. By the very fact of being me, I believed I deserved material things. My mother grew up in a family that didn't have money: six siblings, and later three stepsiblings, with one working parent, the other a drunk. She loved to take me shopping. This was always reflected beneath our Christmas tree – but also throughout the year. She wanted her daughter to have things she never had.

I remember asking her for bell-bottom jeans. It couldn't wait. I had to have them immediately. She was not in the mood to go shopping that day. Just wasn't in the mood. But finally, I convinced her.

I ran my mouth as we left the house, leaping down from the porch as I shut the front door. 'I get all I want!' I sang.

I'm shocked by this.

My mother stopped in her tracks and ordered me back inside. The look on her face still brings me shame.

I wish I could say the story ends there but it doesn't. A few minutes later, and after many apologies, we went to the mall.

Cross opens *Amway* with the testimonies of Amway distributors from around the world. There is no country in the world where Rich DeVos's Compassionate Capitalism does not work, Cross says.

'I was a salaried man working in a company for eight years,' says Kaoru Nakajima, Japan's first Amway Crown Ambassador. 'Now I am my own boss. Now I am free. Now I am selling products that make me proud.'

Unfulfilled in your current job? Feeling trapped? Amway frees you.

Shy introvert? Learn to be more outgoing with Amway.

Bored with your life? Feeling adrift? Amway gives you purpose.

How do they sell their products? Not in retail stores – Amway distributors can only sell their products directly to the public, or to other Amway distributors. This may not seem so bad until one considers that the price point for many Amway products is about twice that of similar products found in retail stores. Or that in blind tests, Amway products consistently score poorly.

So, how is it that Amway continues to profit? Cross quotes James W. Robinson, author of *Empire of Freedom: The Amway Story*:

> The export lifeblood of some countries is oil, for others it is cars, or diamonds, or food . . . America's most precious export is not a commodity, natural resource, or manufactured product, but an *idea:* putting free enterprise in the hands of the common man and woman.

Listen to the story of Ed Johnson. Ed's family lost everything when the recession hit San Antonio in the 1980s. Ed's son showed him The Plan in 1992 and, after some initial resistance from Ed's wife, soon the whole family was working hard to achieve their dreams the American way. Then tragedy struck. Just as he was qualifying for Diamond, Ed had to undergo emergency surgery to remove a brain tumor. Then he had to undergo radiation therapy. Did Ed let this stop him? Of course he didn't. He 'showed his mettle' and his 'desire to get on with his life' by prospecting three doctors and six nurses while he was in the hospital recovering from brain cancer treatment – enabling the Johnsons to go Diamond sixty-two months after joining Amway.

'Although Ed's challenges would have devastated most families, the Johnsons saw them as an opportunity to pull together,' Cross says.

'There are no excuses,' he quotes Ed as saying. 'Just performance.'

M y parents more or less broke even in Amway. I learned recently that my mom was against it from the start. She believed it was a cult, and wasn't happy about giving their time and money to it. She hated Amway's right-wing political propaganda and evangelical bullying. She hated that it kept the two of them from spending time with me. 'She wasn't going to leave me,' my dad says. 'But there was tension because she didn't want to go do these things.' In four years, they built up their downline to something like forty people. It was a cumbersome organization but the people they were working with, save for one, were all honest. A lot of them had families we'd grown close to – the kids were my friends. I'd go to their houses on the weekends, and after school, and whenever my parents needed a babysitter. After we left Amway, I never saw them again.

In the beginning, my parents put between ten and fifteen hours a week into their business – per the company's recommendation. But over time, my dad's enthusiasm began to wear off. 'You say to yourself, "What the hell for?" So that somebody can come in and then not return your calls? You take them to a meeting and there's a jerk up there who's embarrassing?'

The embarrassing jerk was my parents' upline, Vincent, who had Emerald status. My dad says, 'He was a creepy guy, just an incredibly creepy guy. I don't know how else to describe him . . . You actually felt, after being around the guy, that you needed to take a shower.' This is not the man who brought my dad in, but the man above him. He was what The Business calls a 'phony Emerald'. To meet the criteria for the Pin Level, he'd force the people in his organization to order extra product in order to grow his volume and push him across the finish line each month – not that he turned much of a profit doing so, as he had to pass it all on to his own upline. 'Well, the Emerald pin doesn't mean anything unless your organization is solid,' said my dad. 'So you got a pin – you're not making the money.'

It was hard enough to get people to sign up for Amway. Most people had heard of the company and believed it was a pyramid scheme. In fact, part of showing The Plan was that you didn't even tell people it was Amway until the very end of your presentation – then you signed them up on the spot. If you couldn't sign them up right then, you invited them to a meeting. Most of the time, even though you told them not to talk to anybody about Amway before the meeting, they'd go to their brother-in-law, who would tell them it was crap. 'And if they make it to the meeting, this guy stands up there and is a complete ass,' says my dad. 'And the people that you encouraged and cajoled, they take a look at you and say, "*What*?" And then they don't return your phone call.'

I think of my family's time in Amway as achievement tourism. We left reality for a moment and believed the impossible was possible. My dad still wonders if there's more he could have done, if there's a way for him to have succeeded in Amway – admitting in the next breath that there isn't. My parents tried everything. At each turn, the people who were supposed to be helping them actually stood in their way. They built dreams and worked to achieve them, but the only people who benefited from their work were the people already on top.

The dreams I built in Amway don't appeal to me anymore. I find them claustrophobic – ultimately they made the walls close in on my family as we reduced our visions for ourselves to what we owned rather than who we were and how we lived our lives. But every time I drive past the Bayou Club, I can't help wondering what it would have been like to go Diamond. That highest Pin Level – above Silver, Gold, Platinum, Ruby, Pearl, Sapphire and Emerald – Diamond status was what I had craved. It was what I'd believed was success.

In 2010, Amway reached a settlement valued at $100 million in a California class action lawsuit filed by three former distributors who claimed the company was operating as a pyramid scheme. The company announced in a letter to its employees that it was taking action to address many of the concerns raised in the case. A year after settling the California case, Amway offices in India were raided for the second time. The following year, they were raided again, and the CEO of Amway India was arrested for fraud. In 2014, Founders Crown Ambassadors Barry Chi and Holly Chen, who run the biggest Amway distributorship in the world based in Taiwan, were sued by nine Chinese immigrants in the southern California region who claimed that although Chi and Chen promised they could make potentially millions in commissions, Amway business owners make closer to $200 a month.

Some things never change. ∎

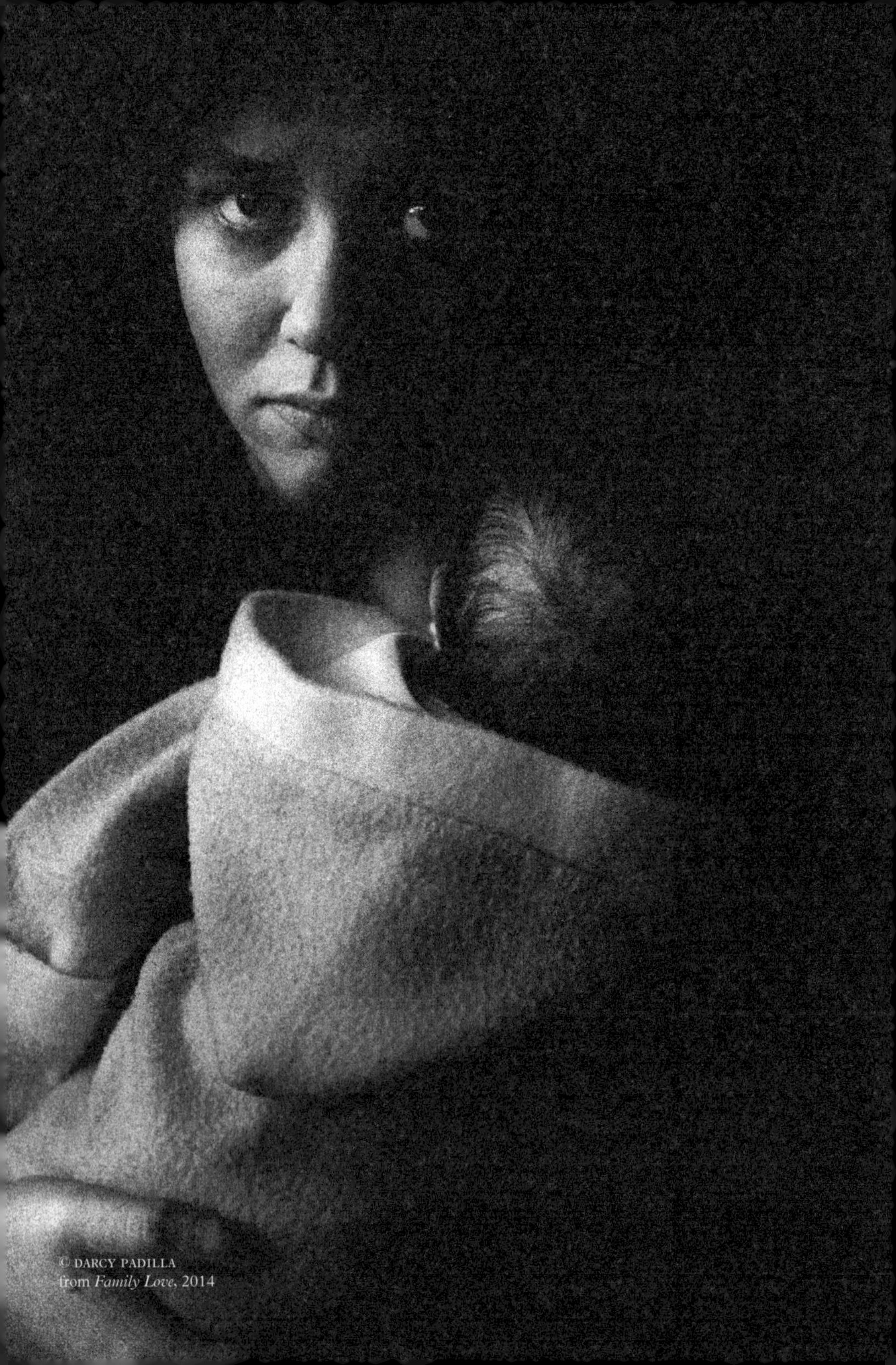

from *Family Love*, 2014

JULIE'S LIFE

Emmanuel Carrère

TRANSLATED FROM THE FRENCH BY LINDA COVERDALE

1

The Tenderloin district near 6th Street in downtown San Francisco is a black ghetto, a crack market, such a hotbed of poverty and crime that you even see people smoking cigarettes out in public. Most hotels there work with social services and receive the tenants' benefits directly, to ensure that their rooms are paid for before they run out to score. In the early nineties, when hospitals were overcrowded at the height of the Aids epidemic, these hotels also served as annexes for patients beyond all help except their daily morphine. Such a place was the Ambassador Hotel, which the young photographer Darcy Padilla began visiting in 1992 while documenting a physician on his rounds. When that project was over, she returned on her own to photograph the patients with whom she had developed a rapport. Even today, she still speaks with emotion about Dorian, the transsexual so proud of her breasts, Diane, who weighed only sixty-five pounds, and Steven, who was so frightened of dying alone that Darcy wished she could promise to be with him when the time came, but she knew better than to make risky promises like that and though she spent several hours a day reading to him from the book of short stories she'd given him and feeding him vanilla ice cream, the only thing he could still stomach, Steven did indeed die alone one night at 3 a.m., undoubtedly in horror and despair, while Darcy slept peacefully with her then boyfriend seven or eight blocks away.

The stories of Dorian, Diane, Steven and many others are much alike: running away very young from poor and violent families to drugs, prostitution and life on the streets, and then the devastating disease that turned them into bags of bones and open sores before dragging them to the end, that black pit waiting in a sordid room at the Ambassador Hotel. The people who were twenty or thirty years old when she photographed them are all dead now and there is no one to remember them but Darcy, who keeps hundreds of pictures of each one in boxes labeled with their names. These black-and-white snapshots that show them laughing and crying, displaying their wounds and their fears and miseries, may be all that is left of their lives. The book Darcy had been dreaming of back then was a gallery of portraits called *Separate Lives, Different Worlds: Living Poor in Urban America*. When she met Julie, she had no way of knowing she would spend the next eighteen years recording her life all the way to her death.

Julie and Jack were only two of many tenants at the Ambassador, yet they stood out because although both were HIV-positive, they were not sick and had even just had a baby. Julie was then nineteen, Jack twenty-one, and Rachel was eight days old. Julie spent most of her days with Rachel in the hotel lobby, where she felt better than in their flea-infested room. There she sat, in the armchair near the picture window overlooking the street, her fly wide open on a belly still swollen from pregnancy. She was surly, mistrustful, and anyone who spoke to her got told to fuck off. But when Darcy asked, gently and politely, if she might take pictures of her baby, whom no one had even thought to photograph, Julie warmed up a little. Despite her reluctance to sign anything, she did okay the release form Darcy handed her: okay to get her picture taken, okay to publish the photos someday. Jack arrived, and when he took Rachel in his arms, it was touching to see how earnestly and clumsily he tried to behave like a fond new father. In the end, the couple were pleased to have their pictures taken as proud, young parents. It was as if they were normal people, as if they had a family. On that January day in 1993, Darcy became their family.

2

Darcy Padilla is a lovely and energetic woman. At our first meeting, when her confident beauty and evident ease with her place in the world swiftly persuaded me that she came from a privileged background, she laughed. 'What do you think?' she asked Andy, her partner. 'Working or lower-middle class? Let's say lower-lower-middle class.' Her father was a social worker of Mexican descent; her mother, a hospital cafeteria lady. In the small inland California towns where Darcy and her brother grew up, they were always the brown kids, the little Chicanos – and always top of the class. Catholic schools, meritocracies, strong principles. When ten-year-old Darcy ran for student council, her father scoffed at her campaign slogan, VOTE FOR DARCY PADILLA. 'You can do better, my girl, and while you're at it, get this – there are two kinds of politicians: those who make promises they don't keep, and those who won't promise what they're not sure they can deliver. The choice is yours.' She remembered this when Steven tried to make her swear that she would be holding his hand when he died.

Her major accomplishment as a student councilor – because of course she was elected – was to publish a class yearbook, for which she took the photos. From the moment she picked up that little automatic camera, Darcy knew what she wanted to do in life, and she did it. I'll skip her further studies (brilliant), the nothing jobs, the internships. I will point out, however, that when she was twenty she worked only three months as an intern at *The New York Times* before they offered her a position. She turned it down, despite the security it represented, because full-time employment would have kept her from doing what she wanted, the way she wanted.

The first photoessay she sold was about a homeless woman living in cardboard boxes near a bus station. She went on to photograph street children in Guatemala, a shelter for battered women and prison inmates with Aids. Poverty is her subject: if she were sent to cover a Russian oligarch's birthday in Courchevel, I believe she would manage to come back with pictures of people without teeth sniffing glue behind the chairlifts or staggering around the street talking to themselves. These are the people she wants to stand up for, but she knows where to draw the line. As a child she saw poverty close up: Mr Padilla, as he was respectfully known, shouldered the responsibility for all the drug addicts and juvenile delinquents wherever her family lived, and Darcy has no desire to put herself in any danger. Nan Goldin she is not: none of her close friends has died of Aids, she has never smoked a single joint, she is upbeat, athletic, pays attention to what she eats and lives in a nice, well-organized apartment. I think being anchored in this perfectly straight life is what allows her to take charge so capably of the tattered lives of people like Julie. She gets close to them, constantly wondering what it's like to be in their place, but she stays in hers. As my good friend Judge Étienne Rigal[1] would say – it is the highest compliment he can pay any human being – she knows where she stands.

3

One day, after a vicious quarrel with her husband, Julie's seventeen-year-old mother picked up her six-month-old baby and left their upcountry Alaskan town for California, in search of a

---

[1] One of the protagonists in *Other Lives but Mine* by Emmanuel Carrère.

better life. She did not find one. Alcoholic and unable to work, she drifted through chance encounters with men who were willing to give her and her little girl shelter for a while. One of them, who'd lasted long enough for Julie to think of him as her stepfather, raped her when she was a teenager. It was her turn to run away. She did not see her mother again, and never learned what happened to her. At fourteen, Julie was living on the streets getting hooked on alcohol and amphetamines. When she met Jack, whose story was much the same as hers, he was hustling. They discovered they were HIV-positive during a pregnancy check-up, but they weren't sick yet, so they didn't much care. They figured they would die young anyway – everyone around them was dying young – and they were completely unable to imagine a future for themselves. In the meantime, the baby Rachel gave them a reason to live. They were proud of her, loved her, would have liked to be good parents, but hadn't a clue what that was, being good parents. No one had ever shown them how to do that. Darcy, who had learned early on to make her bed and tidy up her bedroom, was appalled by the grungy chaos in their place. At first the couple didn't dare invite her into their home, and I was upset as well when I saw a photo of Rachel sleeping with her head next to a pillow pockmarked with cigarette burns, holes showing that her mother or father, nodding off while smoking, had not once but a hundred times almost set fire to the bed where their two-year-old daughter lay asleep.

B ut Julie was trying: she wanted to quit speed and it was because Jack wouldn't, or couldn't, that they broke up. Speed turned him into such a wild animal that simply the way he walked – Darcy did an impression for me – frightened people in the street. He did not go far, just to another hotel a few blocks away, but the scope of their lives was so reduced that he might as well have moved to the East Coast, and they lost track of each other. Darcy continued to see Julie and Rachel, and Julie used to introduce her proudly as 'my photographer'. She was pleased by the fact that Darcy gave her prints and made her little photo albums. Of course the pictures she preferred were the happy ones, of children and not, as she joked, 'the ones you like', where she looked like a wreck. A new couple had moved into the hotel, again HIV-positive addicts but not sick, and in that milieu they were the lucky ones. They had two children, whom Julie took care of when the parents were too strung out, and she liked to have Darcy come over on those days, when there were three little kids running up and down the stairs and wrestling on the beds. They'd all go together to a McDonald's, where Darcy would watch them wolf down the burgers she bought them, eating nothing herself, being firmly opposed to junk food, a squeamishness that gave Julie hysterics and became a favorite joke between them. One day Darcy invited them to a little Vietnamese restaurant that Julie had never even thought of trying, even though it was just across the street from the hotel. The place still exists. I went there with Darcy and she told me that she'd tried to pay for their meal with her credit card but the owner would only take cash. 'Okay,' she'd said, 'I'll come back tomorrow to pay you,' and she remembers Julie's astonishment, first because Darcy inspired such trust that a man would give her credit instead of calling the police, and second because Darcy actually went back the next day to pay her bill.

As a freelance photographer just starting out at the time, Darcy was living hand to mouth, but she was aware that even with her money problems she was infinitely better off – after all, she had a future – than anyone she knew in the Tenderloin. She always gave as much as she could to the homeless and never behaved as if there were no difference between their lives. It was only when Darcy told Julie about her troubles with boyfriends and her reportage work in mysterious, far-off countries Julie had never even heard of that the simple, human sympathy between them began to make up for any impossible pretence of equality. Julie had her own stories to tell too, with her particular brand of blunt and sarcastic humor. She was haunted by the idea that she would turn out like her mother, alcoholic and neglectful, and that Rachel's life would become as rotten as her own. Darcy listened quietly, offering no protest or reassurance, and when Julie told her she was pregnant again, without knowing which one-night stand was the father, Darcy did not pretend to find this wonderful news. She did, however, support Julie during her pregnancy, once she'd decided to keep the child. She was present, with Rachel, during the birth, which she photographed, and she accompanied Julie when she registered baby Tommy's birth. She took the kids to the clinic when they were sick and Julie didn't dare to go herself, rightly fearing that being seen high could cost her the custody of her kids. Darcy never invited Julie to her home, though, and Julie, who was smart in her own way, never asked why not.

4

In 1997 Julie met Paul. They moved to Stockton, a working-class city some 125 miles from San Francisco, with Julie's two children. Darcy lost touch with her. She wanted to believe that Julie had settled into something like stability as a suburban housewife, a less-than-perfect life, perhaps, but one far preferable to the massive disaster of the Tenderloin. Then one night she received a panicky phone call: Julie was in hospital after a miscarriage, and the police had come to tell her that Paul had been arrested for abusing her son Tommy. Julie had refused to believe it, at first. They'd shoved the report and photos under her nose: bruises, wounds, a face caked with vomit. When she got out of the hospital, Paul was in prison and the two children were in the custody of social services. She was allowed to visit them, but could not take them home yet. Not yet, fine, but when? That wasn't clear. The counselors were evasive, and while Julie knew that calling them bastards and assholes made things worse, she just couldn't help herself. Alone in Stockton, she was losing ground, and feared losing her mind. For the first time, she began hounding Darcy. She would wake her in the middle of the night, even threatening to kill herself, but what she really wanted was for Darcy to adopt Rachel and Tommy. Exasperated, Darcy finally told her that if the children had been removed, it was her own fault. 'Fuck you', said Julie, and hung up. If Julie had never contacted her again, Darcy honestly thinks she would not have gone looking for her: she had truly become too difficult to deal with. But Julie did call back, after sulking for a week, with a new worry to report: she had no idea where Jack was. The last time she'd seen him, a few months earlier, he had not been doing well. Darcy called the hospitals, tapped into her network of doctors and social workers, and located Jack at a hospice in San Francisco, in the last stages of Aids. A bus ticket from Stockton to San Francisco cost twenty dollars, which Julie did not have, so Darcy paid for her few visits. On Jack's bedside table were photos taken by Darcy of the children. He asked for Rachel with heartbreaking insistence, but Julie couldn't bring herself to tell him that Tommy and Rachel had been taken away from her. She kept putting him off, saying that Rachel was at school, that she would bring her next time. Jack died without seeing his daughter again: she was the only gift, he said, that life had ever given him.

5

During the first five years of documenting urban poverty, Darcy's grand project had come together around the figure of Julie, and the grant application she submitted to the Soros Foundation in 1998 was entitled 'Birth and Death Certificates'. She got the grant, previously awarded to Gilles Peress and Bruce Davidson, two stars of the Magnum Agency. Darcy flew to New York, where at a cocktail reception in her honor she noticed a dark-eyed, handsome young man staring at her intently. The handsome young man's name was Andy and, after finishing his studies in economics, he had gone to work for an NGO. A Puerto Rican from the Bronx, he came from a world similar to her own, and with the same values, but Andy was more reserved, with a thoughtfulness and poise in quiet contrast with Darcy's exuberance. While telling me how they had met, Andy said, 'You must have noticed that when Darcy's in a room, all eyes are on her, she's someone you just can't miss.' That aura intimidated him, but what made him think he still had a chance with her was how perfectly natural she seemed, with none of the art-world airs or bravado he associated with photographers. At first things were complicated for them, with him in New York and her in San Francisco, but after two years he left his job and city to join her, not only moving in with her but becoming her professional partner: her agent, accountant, assistant and then the designer and manager of her website. The division of labor is simple: she takes photos, he takes care of the rest, and apparently it works because after twelve years they are still together. They hope it will last forever, and so do I.

At almost the same time as Darcy, Julie met someone, too. Not at a Soros Foundation reception, but at rehab, attending a program neither of them would finish. Although at first Darcy wouldn't have bet a penny on Julie's relationship with Jason, twelve years later, he was still there. As a teenager Jason had fled his parents' home in Portland, Oregon, to live on the streets: drugs, prostitution, HIV – the usual trinity. Plus, in his case, a low IQ and a history of bipolar tendencies, for which he received disability benefits. As he was considered incapable of reliably receiving and managing those benefits, he needed help, and Julie quickly became his adult referent. In a touching series of photos, he looks as happy as a child on Christmas morning in front of Julie, who gravely counts his monthly pension and gives him several bills to buy himself a few hours of fun in his hard-luck life. He reminded me of the simple Lennie in *Of Mice and Men,* and Julie, who had never in her life been anyone's boss, bossed him around the way George did Lennie. Like Lennie, Jason wasn't a bad person, but he could be brutal – and possibly dangerous, according to Darcy. 'Look how he treats their cat,' she told me, shocked, showing me a photo of Jason gripping it behind its shoulders. Well, Andy would never do that, and I'm certain that no cat anywhere is more cosseted than Pablo, the angora that reigns over their attractive apartment on Broderick Street.

6

Julie never took any contraceptive precautions. She knew it was possible to have an abortion, but only in theory, the way you know it's possible to go to the moon. Between 1993 and 2008 she had six children, Rachel and Tommy at the beginning, Elyssa at the end. They were the only babies she ever had in her care. The three others were removed at birth by social services, with good reason, but Julie was crushed anyway. She knew that her life was a catastrophe, that she'd blown everything and was not likely to make a go of it. The only thing she would have liked to get right – and now considered herself capable of doing – was to raise a child who might turn out a little better than she had. Stubbornly signing up for rehab programs she never completed, Julie lived in the hope of earning a certificate proving that she had changed and could now be trusted. She longed to get Rachel and Tommy back, but after she and Jason hooked up they returned to San Francisco, to that sinister Tenderloin where life always seemed to dump her, and Stockton was too far, the bus trip too expensive, and Julie too out of it to keep visiting the kids. 'I'm going, I'm going to go,' she used to say, 'I'm going to take them presents' – but she didn't go, and on the day her case was to be decided she never showed up, so she permanently lost parental rights and the two children were handed over to an adoption center. She never saw them again or learned what happened to them. When notified of that decision, she was once again as big as a beach ball, pregnant by Jason, and became so terrified that this child would be taken away as well that the morning after the birth she and Jason simply wrapped the infant in a baby blanket and fled the hospital. Darcy, who had photographed the delivery, was promptly visited by the police who were looking for them. She began looking as well, hoping to find the fugitives first, to talk some sense into them. After two or three days of intense confusion, sleepless nights, frantic phone calls, meetings and unsuccessful mediations, the parents were arrested as kidnappers and their little girl, Jordan, was handed over – as they had dreaded – to social services, which swiftly put her up for adoption. Julie and Jason were sentenced to a year in prison. They served nine months, during which Darcy visited them regularly. Released, they went back to their life of poverty in the Tenderloin. Two more children were born, Ryan in 2001 and Jason Jr in 2002. Both of them were taken so quickly from the delivery room to the adoption center that Julie barely had a moment to hold either one in her arms. Deeply depressed, she and Jason hardly left their bed, hemmed in by piles of fast-food debris and the pitiful junk the very poor have for possessions. Julie spent her days drinking while Jason smoked weed, and the rhythms of their addictions, the moments of exaltation and the inevitable crashes, did not mesh well together. They hid away like that for two years, and Darcy didn't see much of them.

That was partly because she was quite busy. To increase their income, Andy had suggested that she take up wedding photography, so almost every weekend from then on Darcy was taking color pictures of couples promising mutual love, support and fidelity, surrounded by smiling families sufficiently well-off to afford her services, which do not come cheaply. Thanks to this new venture, Darcy could spend the week taking black-and-white photos of the homeless and submitting each stage of her work-in-progress to prestigious foundations: after Soros came Getty, and after Getty, the Guggenheim, each awarding their grants with the congratulations of the selection committee.

7

While preparing her application for one of the grants, Darcy searched online for articles about Jordan's kidnapping, and googled Julie's name. To her astonishment, she came across a classified notice: 'If you are Julie Baird, born 10 October 1973, in Anchorage, Alaska, call me, I'm looking for you.' Heart pounding, Darcy did call: it was Julie's father. After Julie's mother had disappeared with the baby, he had searched for them desperately before finally losing heart. The new resources of the Internet had inspired him to post his notice – and bingo: a call from a photographer in San Francisco who knew his daughter! Then things happened fast, so fast that, to her great regret, Darcy was unable to witness their reunion. She had accepted an assignment about teenage Mexican gangs in Los Angeles, it was all arranged, and Julie herself would not wait: her father was inviting her home to Alaska, where he still lived, and he was sending her and Jason plane tickets.

Julie left in a complete tangle of exhilaration and anguish, dreaming of a new life with this family she did not know, appalled at the idea of their disappointment – perhaps even their rejection – when they'd see her get off the plane as the wreck she knew she was. Darcy did her best, explaining by email and phone that the thirty-one years since baby Julie had left Alaska had been hard for her. And then Darcy went off to Los Angeles, where she got caught up in her work, as she always does. When she came home three weeks later, the news was not good. Julie had hardly arrived to meet her relatives before she became ill and was hospitalized in Anchorage. Darcy took the first plane out. One look at Julie was enough: no longer just HIV-positive, she had Aids, and what really terrified Julie wasn't dying, it was that her father would find out why. Not daring to tell him, Julie counted on Darcy for that, and, true to form, she took on the job.

Bill Baird, the father, is the big man wearing a lumberjack shirt and tethered to the breathing apparatus visible in the photographs. Darcy liked him right away, and he liked her right back. She says he was a good man. He wept, understood, blamed himself. He was happy to have found his daughter again, unhappy to have found her in that state, but she was his daughter, he loved her, junkie, sick, whatever, he would nurse and take care of her.

Julie pulled through that time, but her life had tipped over the line into illness. She had lost sixty-six pounds and at the age of thirty-one, she looked fifty. Untreatable lesions in her palate and esophagus made her appear to chew endlessly – in a twitching, angry way, and even Jason, undemanding as he was on the question of feminine allure, admitted that this had taken some getting used to. Bill Baird drove them both back to Valdez, where he lived. An hour by plane from Anchorage, weather permitting, or a ten-hour drive, the city of Valdez is cut off from just about everything. Its two thousand citizens live off fishing and the fish cannery, and there is one pizzeria, where Bill was the cook until he retired. He had a second family in Valdez, and his four grown children were openly wary of this scarecrow introduced to them as their half-sister. Word quickly spread that she and Jason had Aids, which did not warm up their welcome. On the other hand, life in Valdez isn't expensive, the state pays people to live there, and that money, added to Jason's disability pension, allowed them to rent a small apartment, by far the finest in the wretched series of their homes.

Bill stopped by every day to see his daughter and took her for long car rides. He showed her the glaciers, the lakes, the eagles, the wild natural landscapes where she might have grown up and perhaps have led a quiet, simple life if her crazy mother hadn't carried her off, and Julie told him, in bits and pieces, about the dreadful life she'd had instead in the jungle of city slums. Through kindness, naiveté, or simply because you can't settle into absolute despair, Bill acted as if it were possible to start over again. He talked about a new beginning.

Then he died of a heart attack. Without him, there was no reason to stay in Valdez. Jason, however, really liked Alaska. He liked the prospect of hunting and fishing, of wide-open spaces and especially of having a gun. At Bill's funeral, they met his brother, another great guy, whom everyone called Uncle Mike and who lived with his wife, Aunt Rita, in a kind of cabin out in the woods near the town of Palmer. Not far from their place was an abandoned trailer on land used more or less as a dump, but no one claimed it, so Jason and Julie went to ground there, into the wild. No electricity, no running water, but no neighbors either, except elk and bears, and they could always take an occasional shower at Mike and Rita's cabin. Despite its lack of creature comforts, Darcy approved of this new place, first off because Palmer is only an hour from Anchorage and its hospital, where Julie would inevitably be spending more and more time, and also, selfishly, because she dreaded the ten-hour drive to Valdez, alone at the wheel of a rental car, sometimes without seeing a single soul along the way.

8

E ven though she'd never gotten over losing her children, Julie did not want another baby – it wasn't worth it, just to have the little thing then watch its mother die. But Jason insisted. Having lived for ten years completely dependent on Julie, he'd come to believe that his emotional and sexual life would die with her, and he wanted, as he put it, to have 'something of his own' when she was gone. Julie lit into him: 'Something? A child isn't a something!' It made no difference; she ended up pregnant. And it was during this pregnancy that another of those new miracles occurred, the ones the Internet has made so commonplace. In the autumn of 2007, Darcy received a call from someone named Karen, who introduced herself as the adoptive mother of Zach, the child Julie and Jason had registered as Jason Jr before he was taken away from them in 2002. When Darcy first told me the story, some things seemed so unbelievable that I asked her to repeat this next part: Karen told her that five-year-old Zach did know he was adopted, but knew nothing about his biological parents – and yet in dream after dream he'd seen them seriously ill up in the Far North, surrounded by bears. His parents were calling to him, and his increasing anxiety had prompted Karen to search for them. Thanks initially to a careless records clerk, and then through Darcy's website, she had found them. Once again, Darcy played go-between, deploying endless euphemisms to put Julie and Jason's sorry lives in the best possible light, while admitting that they had Aids.

When she flew to Anchorage, where Julie was about to give birth, Darcy brought a thoughtful, moving letter from Karen, and one from Zach himself, which said: 'Mommy, I love you. I have good parents but I would like to know you someday.' Darcy took pictures of Julie reading those letters, bursting into tears, then smoking frantically outside to get a grip on herself. Elyssa was born a few days later. Jason had been so afraid Julie would die on the operating table that he had not witnessed the birth, a C-section. As for Darcy, she was there as usual. The newborn was tucked right next to her mother, but this was not 'as usual': no one came to spirit the baby away. Elyssa was the only one of Julie and Jason's children they were able to take home. For the first time, thanks to Uncle Mike and Aunt Rita, they were prepared, equipped: they had a little crib, a car seat, diapers and bottles, and while they certainly were no one's idea of model young parents, it was in that role and setting a few weeks later that they welcomed Zach, the son they had lost six years earlier.

Darcy, who was escorting Karen and Zach, remembers the visit as an occasion of almost suffocating uneasiness. Everyone was expecting so much, and nothing happened. Well, not much except awkwardness and stilted conversation. Julie had lectured Jason at length about behaving himself, making a good impression, not cursing – and then he was the only person who lightened things up a bit, by playing video games with Zach, tossing him up in the air and making him laugh a little. Although not much of a father, as a sort of silly, clowning-around big brother, he wound up reassuring the little boy, whose anxious fantasies had cast his real parents as violent, dangerous people who might hurt or even kill him.

A fter Karen and Zach left, there was something of a stunned lull. Darcy was so tense that she remembers doing something quite unlike her. When Julie – with the usual mumbling and grinding of teeth – persisted in the wooden, artificial chatter she'd affected all through the visit, Darcy blew up. 'Come on, Julie, stop pretending!' She pushed her to admit that the visit had actually gone really badly and that she felt like a complete shit. Then Julie fell apart, saying over and over that Karen was a wonderful woman, that of course she was happy Zach had a good mother, but that she wanted to die because she'd never been able to be that good mother herself; that she really would have preferred Zach to be unhappy so he'd have wanted to come back to her and that yes, Darcy, all right: she was a complete shit. Jason went over and wrapped his arms around her. Darcy took a picture of them like that: it isn't the most striking of her photos, but I think it's one of the images that moves me the most.

9

T hat last year, Julie was hospitalized several times, and each time she came out weaker than when she'd gone in. At home she lay exhausted on the couch, unable to carry Elyssa anymore. Strung out more than half the time, Jason fooled around with a plastic toy gun but still made sure Julie took her thirty-four daily pills on schedule. They didn't do much good. Her pain was increasing and she was literally coming apart at the seams. She went through great waves of bitterness, railing at the fucking idiocy of having had Elyssa, convinced that Jason would never manage to take care of her on his own, but she also experienced brief flushes of gaiety, especially when Darcy was there. It tickled her no end, for example, that Darcy, so finicky about food, had to have Kentucky Fried Chicken like everyone else when she was at their place – and the best part for her was that it was such an old joke between them. That's no small thing, knowing someone long enough to have an old joke in common. It did not take much time to tally up the good things she'd had in life, but still, there had been Darcy. The same shit without her would have been worse, because no one else would ever have known about it. Leaving Elyssa with Uncle Mike and Aunt Rita one evening, Julie, Jason and Darcy went out for margaritas. At the bar Julie winked at Darcy and said, 'You know what? We should take a vacation, just us girls.'

'And where would you like to go?'

'Oh, I dunno . . . Brazil.'

'Brazil?' exclaimed Darcy, and because she had adjusted to Julie's brand of caustic humor over the years, she added, 'So you see yourself on the beach, do you, in a bikini?' The two of them howled themselves dizzy, and after brief puzzlement, Jason joined in – but then kept on laughing. That crack had made his day. Julie in a bikini: Woo-hoo!

10

Darcy and Andy were working at home when the phone rang one September afternoon in 2010. Julie's breathing problems had become so severe that she'd been taken to the hospital, and Aunt Rita was calling in tears to tell them what the doctor had just said: 'We can't do anything more for her now. Take her back home and prepare for the end-of-life procedure.' Darcy hung up and began to cry. Andy hugged her for a long time. He had never met Julie, would not ever meet her, and if Darcy had been a psychoanalyst he would not have met her patients either. But he'd known about Julie as long as he had known Darcy, and his heart was broken, too. They went out to walk in silence for a while in Alta Plaza Park, which overlooks their pleasant neighborhood and offers a view of San Francisco's hills rolling all the way to the ocean. Then they went home to get the plane ticket.

Darcy spent the whole trip wondering if she would take pictures of Julie dying. Wondering if Julie and Jason would want that and if she, Darcy, would have the strength. In the end, she did, without the question ever even arising: at that point, after eighteen years of Julie and Darcy's strange kind of collaboration, why not see it through to the finish . . . The file containing these last photos is labeled julie.end and I don't see what there is to add here, except that Darcy, who is not religious, prayed that Julie's atrocious agony would not last long, though it did: almost three weeks. Julie had sudden panic attacks, believing the room filled with strangers who were going to hurt her. Elyssa kept wanting to play with her. And on the last night Jason, who was watching over her, left her bedside for half an hour to tinker with something, so Julie died alone, during that half-hour, at dawn on 27 September 2010. She was thirty-six years old.

11

A few weeks after the death of its heroine, 'The Julie Project', finally complete, earned Darcy Padilla the prestigious W. Eugene Smith Grant in Humanistic Photography. She was all the more moved in that 'Country Doctor', Smith's celebrated photoessay about a country doctor during the Depression, had been her guide and model when she first set foot in the Ambassador Hotel. So for Darcy, this story has come to a good end. I intend not the slightest irony here, and I sincerely admire her sense of moral purpose, which spares her the misgivings that often afflict artists whose talents and reputations flourish thanks to the misery of others. For Darcy does not see herself so much as an artist, with whatever narcissism that implies, but as a journalist, with the mission of bearing witness. And in her eyes, the story is not over, since with Julie's death, a new chapter begins: her children will be its heroes, and Elyssa first of all. Darcy is raising funds for her education, and if Jason cannot cope with bringing her up or if he dies prematurely, as Darcy and Andy fear, they might adopt her. But Zach and her other four children carry on the story as well. Little Rachel, whom Darcy met when she was eight days old, is now eighteen, but she was six when she saw Julie for the last time, so she ought still to remember her mother. With Karen's help, Darcy is now looking for Rachel, Tommy, Jordan and Ryan, so that she can tell them, if they want, the story of their mother's life.

When Darcy told me this, I wasn't sure it was such a good idea, and I even admit to thinking that no one in the world would ever take the slightest comfort in knowing they'd come from Julie's womb. Then the day before I left, I accompanied Darcy through the Tenderloin where she always returns, where she knows everyone, and where she has begun a new project about the clients of a psychiatric outreach centre that has – unfortunately – just closed. She was looking for someone in particular, whom she had already photographed once but whose address she didn't have, supposing he even had one. So we wandered the streets, questioning various derelicts and punks with dogs, until at last we happened to spot him. He was a boy with a childlike face, trashed by heroin, who, despite a bad case of the shakes, spoke articulately and even with remarkable gentleness. He invited us to his hotel room, which hit me like a nightmare, although Darcy assured me later that Julie's rooms had been much worse. At one point, the boy talked about his mother, who had abandoned him when he was four. 'I don't know where she is,' he said sadly. Then, with the care for words that had struck me from the beginning, he added, 'or who she was. You see, I don't even know what verb tense to use with her. I don't know anything, not where she is, if she's alive or dead. I think . . . probably a prostitute and a junkie, but I don't care about that, I'd like to find out, I would like so badly to know who my mom was, and I'll never know.' When he said that he began to cry, very softly, and it occurred to me that perhaps Darcy was right after all.

The last I heard from Darcy, Jason is serving seventeen years in prison for the sexual abuse of a minor. Four of the children are known to be adopted. The status of the other two is unknown. ■

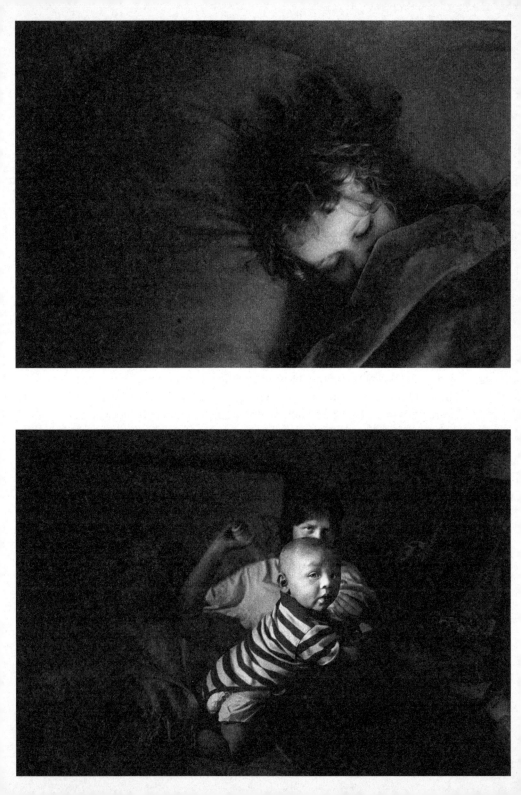

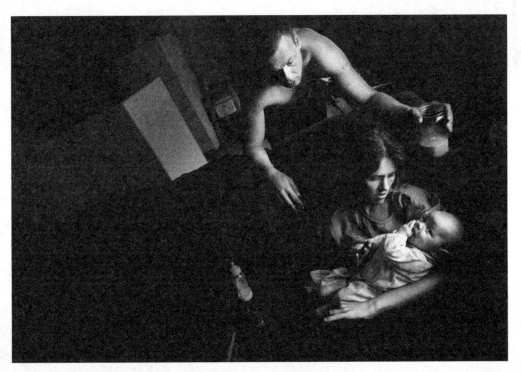

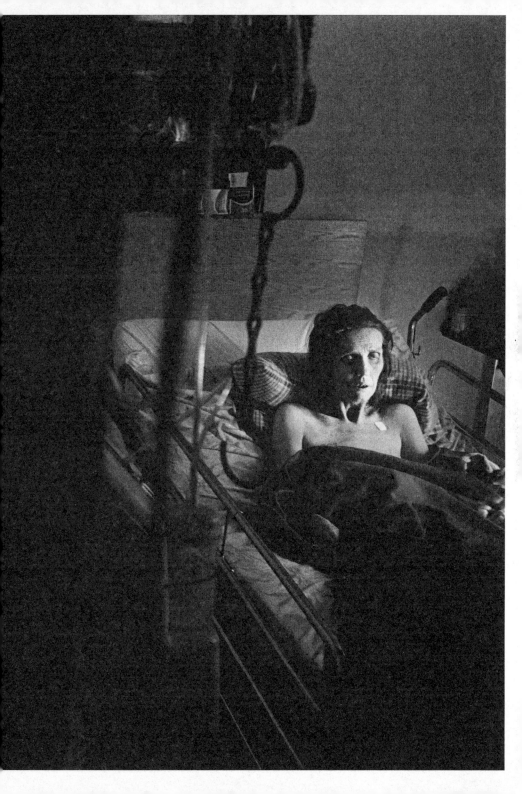

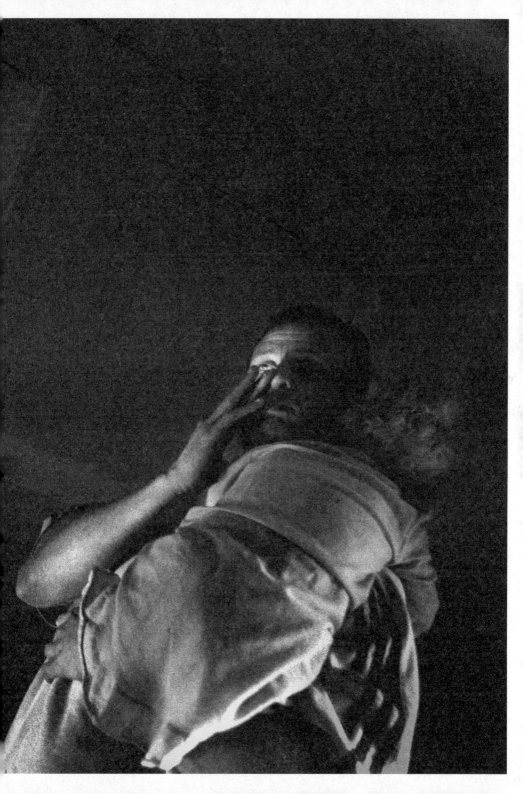

Will Alexander is a Whiting Fellow, a California Arts Council Fellow, and has won a PEN Oakland Award, an American Book Award, as well as the Jackson Poetry Prize. He is the author of nearly thirty books.

Emmanuel Carrère is a novelist, film-maker, journalist and biographer. His books include *Limonov*, *Lives Other Than My Own*, *The Adversary* and *My Life as a Russian Novel*.

Feng Sun Chen lives in Minneapolis and is the author of two poetry collections, *Butcher's Tree* and *The 8th House*.

Ivan Chistyakov was expelled from the Communist Party during the purges of the late 1920s and early 1930s. He was killed during the 1941 German offensive in the Russian province of Tula. *The Diary of a Gulag Prison Guard* is forthcoming by Pegasus Books in the US and Granta Books in the UK.

Linda Coverdale has translated more than eighty books. A Chevalier de l'Ordre des Artes et des Lettres, she has won the 2004 International IMPAC Dublin Literary Award, the 2006 Scott Moncrieff Prize and the 1997 and 2007 French-American Foundation Translation Prize. She lives in Brooklyn.

Ken Follett is the author of over thirty books, including *Edge of Eternity*, *Fall of Giants* and *The Pillars of the Earth*, which was recently adapted into a screenplay. He is currently working on a spy story set in the reign of Queen Elizabeth I.

Sarah Gerard is the author of *Binary Star*. Her essay collection *Sunshine State* is forthcoming in 2017 by Harper

Perennial. Her work has appeared in the *New York Times*, the *Paris Review Daily* and elsewhere. The full version of 'Going Diamond' is published on Granta.com.

Peter Graves is an Honorary Fellow of Scandinavian Studies in the University of Edinburgh.

Eliza Griswold is a poet and journalist and a Berggruen Fellow at Harvard Divinity School.

Matilda Gustavsson is a reporter and a columnist for the Swedish newspaper *Dagens Nyheter*. She is currently working on a novel about the Word of Life movement in Sweden. She lives in Stockholm.

A.M. Homes's most recent book is the novel *May We Be Forgiven*, winner of the 2013 Women's Prize for Fiction. She teaches at Princeton University and lives in New York City.

Lauren Hough was raised in the Family and has lived in seven different countries. She's been an air force airman, a green-aproned barista, a bartender and a stand-up comic. She lives in Austin, Texas.

Françoise Huguier is a documentary photographer. She has been awarded the World Press Photo Prize, the Académie des Beaux-Arts Photography Prize and has twice won the Villa Médicis Hors les Murs Award. She has produced numerous works on Africa, Siberia, Japan, Russia and India. She is also the founder of the Bamako Biennale in Mali, was the chief curator of the Luang Prabang Biennale in Laos in 2010, as well as the 2011 Photoquai Biennale.

Luke Kennard's fifth collection of poems, *Cain*, was published by Penned in the Margins in 2016. He lectures at the University of Birmingham. His first novel, *The Transition*, will be published by 4th Estate in 2017.

Darcy Padilla is a photographer, journalist and lecturer. Her honours include fellowships from the Guggenheim Foundation, Open Society Institute and the W. Eugene Smith Grant in Humanistic Photography. Padilla's recent book, *Family Love*, follows Julie Baird and her family for 21 years – an intimate story of poverty, Aids and social issues.

Kelly Schirmann is a writer, musician and artist from Northern California. She is the author of *Popular Music* and the co-author of *Boyfriend Mountain*. She records music as Sung Mountains and edits Black Cake, a record label for contemporary poetry and other experiments. She lives in Oregon.

Arch Tait was awarded the PEN Literature in Translation prize in 2010 for his translation of *Putin's Russia* by Anna Politkovskaya. He has translated thirty books from the Russian, most recently Mikhail Gorbachev's *The New Russia*.

Aatish Taseer is the author of *The Way Things Were*, shortlisted for the 2016 Jan Michalski Prize for Literature, and *The Temple-goers*, shortlisted for the 2010 Costa First Novel Award. He is a contributing opinion writer for the *International New York Times*. 'The Interpreters' is loosely drawn from a forthcoming work of non-fiction, *The Twice Born*.

Adam Thorpe is a poet, novelist, translator and critic. He is the author of the novel *Ulverton* and of the poetry collection *Voluntary*. He lives in the Cévennes mountains.

Miriam Toews is a Canadian writer. Her novels include *A Complicated Kindness*, *Irma Voth* and most recently *All My Puny Sorrows*, which was shortlisted for the 2015 Folio Prize and the 2015 Wellcome Book Prize. It won the 2015 Canadian Authors Award for Fiction.

Tomas van Houtryve is an artist, photographer and author. In 2006 he was named one of PDN's 30 Emerging Photographers. He was awarded an Alicia Patterson Journalism Fellowship in 2008, and in 2010 he was named the POYi Photographer of the Year. His work has been exhibited solo and in collections around the world.

Lara Vapnyar moved to the US from Russia in 1994. She is the author of three novels and two story collections and the recipient of a Guggenheim Fellowship. Her stories and essays have appeared in the *New Yorker*, the *New York Times*, *Harper's* and *Vogue*. Her most recent novel is *Still Here*.

Javier Zamora was born in El Salvador and migrated to the US when he was nine. He is a 2016–2018 Wallace Stegner Fellow and holds fellowships from the Poetry Foundation, MacDowell and the National Endowment for the Arts. His first poetry collection, *Unaccompanied*, is forthcoming from Copper Canyon Press.